THE
JOURNALIST'S
HANDBOOK

An insider's guide to being a great journalist

Kim Fletcher has worked on Fleet Street since 1981 as a news reporter, feature writer, news editor and editor.

He has been a staff reporter, specialist correspondent and weekly columnist on the *Sunday Times* and the *Daily Telegraph*, news editor and deputy editor of the *Sunday Telegraph* and editor of the *Independent on Sunday*. He is currently editorial director of Telegraph Group Limited, publishers of the *Daily Telegraph* and the *Sunday Telegraph*.

Fletcher has contributed to many other publications and is a frequent broadcaster on national television and radio. Since 2004 he has been chairman of the National Council for the Training of Journalists.

THE
JOURNALIST'S
HANDBOOK

An insider's guide to being a great journalist

KIM FLETCHER

MACMILLAN

First published 2005 by Macmillan
an imprint of Pan Macmillan Ltd
Pan Macmillan, 20 New Wharf Road, London N1 9RR
Basingstoke and Oxford
Associated companies throughout the world
www.panmacmillan.com

ISBN 1 4050 4088 2

Inclusion in *The Journalist's Handbook* is entirely at the author's discretion.
Macmillan Publishers Ltd makes no recommendation whatsoever by the
inclusion or omission of any organization.

While every effort has been made to ensure all of the information
contained in this publication is correct and accurate, the publisher cannot
accept any responsibility for any omissions or errors that may occur or from
any consequences arising therefrom. The publisher would be grateful for
any new or corrected information and will make the appropriate
change at the earliest opportunity.

A CIP catalogue record for this book is available from
the British Library.

Typeset by Intypelibra, London
Printed and bound in Great Britain by
Mackays of Chatham plc, Chatham, Kent

All Pan Macmillan titles are available from www.panmacmillan.com
or from Macmillan Direct on 01256 302699

Contents

Acknowledgements

This book would never have got off the ground without the enthusiasm of Morven Knowles at Macmillan, and Alex Stitt, who runs the Enterprises Department at the *Daily Telegraph*. Journalists are always flattered to be asked to write something, so when they suggested I expand on the media column that appeared each week in the paper, I agreed immediately.

When Morven Knowles gave in to the excitement of newspapers and came down to Canary Wharf to become publisher of Telegraph Books, Georgina Morley and Natasha Martin inherited me at Macmillan. They took me out for a big lunch, where they explained that journalists were the bane of publishers' lives, being lazy, arrogant and incapable of writing to a deadline.

Not me, I said, and vowed to prove them wrong. Despite Natasha Martin's generous encouragement, inspired editing and clever use of the guilt trap, I am not sure that I did so.

Pav Akhtar, a graduate of the *Daily Telegraph* training course, worked most efficiently on creating the contacts pages of this book and charmed editors and writers into passing on their career tips. I thank him and them.

My thanks are due too to my agent, Maggie Pearlstine, who's been waiting four years for a novel but thought this book might jump-start some writing. I fear she thought wrong.

And, of course, I thank all the journalists I have ever met, the good ones, the bad ones, the friendly ones, the ones you'd hide behind a bar stool to avoid. One of them – from the first category – is my wife Sarah Sands, who shames me with her work rate, enthrals me with her prose and runs a 24-hour media tutorial service.

Finally, this book began before the war in Iraq, when journalists were routinely abused for reporting the private lives of politicians, recording the sexual activities of Premier League footballers and spying on celebrity drug-takers. In the war – and in the 'peace' that followed it – journalists risked injury, kidnap and death. Some risked and lost. They showed what a proper trade journalism is, for which we might all thank them.

PART 1

THE INDUSTRY

1

So you want to be a journalist?

There are jobs that are guaranteed to make you admired: no one ever says that being a doctor is a waste of talent. There are jobs that are lucrative: who has ever met an investment banker with no money? There are jobs that are treated with respect: think of teaching.

And then there's journalism.

The *Chambers Dictionary* dignifies journalism with the label 'profession', as in 'the profession of collecting, writing, editing, publishing, etc. news reports and other articles for newspapers, journals, television, radio and related media . . .'

But well-educated members of the professional classes shudder at the idea that their ranks include journalists. People give their lives to journalism, some have given their lives *for* it. But it is a trade, a business, a job.

It is as well to get this right from the start. The Oxford graduate with a double first in Greats who writes leaders for *The Times* and the reporter who left school at sixteen and who now goes under cover to report on massage parlours for the *News of the World* are in the same business. Indeed, they work for the same man – Rupert Murdoch. From the newspaper plant that brings you *The Times* also comes the *Sun*. You don't have to admire or excuse all that is done in the name of journalism, but if you are serious about getting involved in it, you can't get away with pretending you are part of a different, more worthy business.

It may be this roughness at the edges, the fact that it is not quite proper, that gives journalism such appeal. It exudes a faint scent of risk, of mischief, of – we may as well say it now – grubbiness. If you are looking for the kind of job that makes you welcome wherever you go, you'd better stop now. But you can't help feeling that journalists have a lot more fun than trainee solicitors.

Even the National Council for the Training of Journalists, the body that supervises training and decides whether you are competent to call yourself a senior reporter, acknowledges the appeal: 'Newspaper journalism is often seen as glamorous and exciting.' But, before you get carried away with the romance of it all, the Council offers a little warning: 'As with any occupation, success comes only after much hard work and routine activity.'

For many of us, it is the glamour rather than the hard work that formed our earliest impressions. They were encouraged by the film industry. In the early years of Hollywood, producers turned to journalists for scripts and to newspapers for subjects. So it is no surprise that films have helped recruit successive generations of journalists. I know people who work in newspapers today who cite Orson Welles's *Citizen Kane* as a major influence on their choice of career, even though they were born twenty years after it was first screened in 1941. Then there's Billy Wilder's 1951 film *Ace in the Hole*, starring Kirk Douglas as a cynical reporter who tries to manipulate an accident to the advantage of his story. And, famously, *The Front Page*, written for the stage in 1928 by Ben Hecht and Charles MacArthur, who drew on their experiences as reporters in Chicago. It was a big hit on Broadway, became a best-selling book and spawned four Hollywood film adaptations.

In the words of Robert Schmuhl, professor of American studies at the University of Notre Dame, the playwrights created enduring stereotypes of journalism: 'Different times and vastly different technologies notwithstanding, the drive of news competition, the excitement of a big story, and the sense of purposeful fun still animate how journalists think, talk, and act.' Yes indeed, to the point that,

4

if *The Front Page* leaves you cold, you may be making a mistake in looking for a career in journalism.

The technology is changing but the basics stay the same. Here is a job where someone is paying you to see things you would pay to see, to go to places where you couldn't otherwise go; to stand – say – on the fringes of a riot, to watch troops go in, to hear the Prime Minister at the despatch box, to see the fastest runner in the world; to absorb these things, to reproduce and describe them; to race for the phone, the laptop, the satellite link.

The television presenter and sports writer Michael Parkinson started his journalistic career in Barnsley, his home town, and has described how heavily he was influenced by the newspapermen he watched in the black and white Hollywood films of the 1950s. I worked in Barnsley twenty years later for the evening title the *Star* and was pleased to find that this romanticism was still going strong. It was now 1980, but the latest trainee on the *Chronicle* had bought himself a trench coat and a trilby and, having just reached eighteen, had taken to leaning on the bar of the pub rather than hiding at the back. Whenever he opened his wallet to pay for a round of drinks, he'd make sure that the barmaid noticed the press card in it. This, he felt – though we never saw the notion proved – would establish him as a tough-talking, wisecracking ladies' man in the great tradition of *film noir*.

And just as the influence of recycled films might have started to wane, along came an event that defined the power of the press. For the age group looking now towards retirement – men and women in their fifties – the big spur was Watergate, the finest hour of American journalism, when the painstaking work of two reporters on the *Washington Post* led ultimately to the impeachment and resignation of President Richard Nixon in 1974. The film that followed two years later, *All the President's Men*, with Dustin Hoffman and Robert Redford playing the journalists Carl Bernstein and Bob Woodward, encouraged a new generation to turn its backs on proper jobs and head for the glamour, excitement and now power of journalism. Now there was a vogue for investigative reporting, with everyone looking for the story that would bring down, if not a government, at least a local council.

More recently, in 1985, *Defence of the Realm*, with Gabriel Byrne, Denholm Elliot and Greta Scacchi, gave the most realistic account of British newspaper life I have seen on screen, possibly because one of my friends, an experienced Fleet Street reporter, was called in to advise on the detail. Here were the scruffy offices, the battered typewriters, the cynical old reporters and the dirty boozers of the last days of Fleet Street, before we moved out to Canary Wharf office blocks and computer screens. Then the American film *The Paper*, 1994, starring Michael Keaton, Glenn Close and Robert Duvall, captured the American newspaper world with real wit, right down to the insufferable pomposity of the *New York Times* and the vicious competitiveness that underlies the trade. If you find one of these running on television, don't miss it.

The popular BBC1 thriller series *State of Play*, broadcast in 2003, may not have given the most recognizable portrayal of a British broadsheet newspaper, but it did give the most exciting and romantic one, possibly because the clever and entertaining *Guardian* political sketch writer Simon Hoggart worked as an adviser on the show. There were murders, sex scenes, double-crossings, twists and improbable stretches of plot from which the journalists emerged in triumph. The journalists who watched it agreed there were certain inaccuracies, but couldn't help wanting the editor Bill Nighy as their own editor. The serial involved politicians, police and press, but the writer realized that it was the press who were holding the audience's attention and decided to write politicians out of the sequel. *State of Play* ended with the hero journalist deep in the paper's print plant, watching as thousands of copies of his front-page story rolled from the presses around him. If that didn't make you want to be a reporter, nothing would.

There are classic books too – none better, despite its age, than Evelyn Waugh's comic novel *Scoop*, set at the time of the Italian invasion of Abyssinia in 1935 but uncannily descriptive of newspaper journalism today: the same misunderstandings, the same demands from an office that has little idea of the story unfolding on the spot, the same competition between reporters fearful that another has a better story. In 2003 the *Daily Telegraph* journalist W. F. Deedes celebrated his ninetieth birthday not only by continuing to work as a reporter for the *Telegraph* but also by publishing *At War with Waugh*, his account of his experiences alongside Waugh covering that same Abyssinia campaign. Lord Deedes has been a Conservative Cabinet minister and an editor of the *Daily Telegraph*, but neither appealed to him as much as the practice and craft of reporting.

Many other journalists have captured the mischief, madness – and, from time to time, value – of journalism in books, whether writing about newspaper events or their own careers. Sir Max Hastings, the former editor of the *Daily Telegraph* and the *Evening Standard* and a distinguished war correspondent, gave good encouragement to the adventurous in *Going to the Wars*. The American news agency reporter Ed Behr wrote a frank account of international war reporting in *Anyone Here Been Raped and Speaks English?* I knew I had to be a journalist when, half-way through a law degree, I read *Slip-Up*, Anthony Delano's account of the competition to get to the runaway Great Train Robber Ronnie Biggs. In particular I remember his throwaway line on moving to Fleet Street from the provinces, 'not long married to the prettiest girl in town'. This, clearly, was the life for me. There are more earnest and more important books, but if you get no joy from these, you might question whether you should really be a journalist.

Clearly, thousands do. The popularity of the business has risen to the point where the Civil Service, leading law firms and big-paying investment banks, which once expected to cream off the brightest university graduates, complain that too many are heading for journalism instead.

Worse, some of these bright men and women seem to be running off to journalism for no more high-minded reason than the pursuit of fame. According to a survey conducted in 2002, the most popular role models among media students were the show business gossip writers on the *Daily Mirror*, the 3am Girls.

Their popularity reflected a change that was going on at university newspapers and magazines that had taken their cue from national print media increasingly interested in entertainment. The change in student attitudes was noticed by the *Daily Telegraph*, which sponsors annual conferences on student journalism. University newspapers seemed to be publishing less about socio-political issues such as inequality, racism, low pay and asylum and more about socio-social issues such as travel, pop and gossip. The student newspaper editors defended this on the basis that they were writing what their peer group wanted to read, though they did not seem too happy about it. This, you will find, is a common complaint among journalists. The journalists want to give their readers what the journalists think is important; the readers want to read what the readers like.

Jack Doyle, who was then editor of *Student Direct* in Manchester, told the *Telegraph* that his contemporaries read tabloid rather than broadsheet newspapers. The show business gossip magazine *Heat* was the most popular read of all.

Jan Webster, a former editor of Sheffield University's *Steel Press*, explained how things had changed: 'Our paper used to boast a fantastic news team. Now, many of those joining the paper think journalism is swanning around talking to celebs. Many of them don't want to make a phone call and are scared to talk to student union officers. What you have now are people who want to write down their opinions. It's not journalism.'

But if that is what papers want now, it surely *is* journalism. When the former *Daily Mirror* editor Piers Morgan decided his paper was threatening to drown in show business froth, he announced a crusade to return to a more challenging, cerebral form of journalism. Sadly, his readers didn't like it and began to desert the paper. The froth came back.

But don't worry. If you want to be serious, there are still papers ready to be as serious as you want. And if, like those questioned in the survey, it is show business you yearn for, be warned that there are plenty of people who believe that reporting has a more important function.

That function, without wishing to sound too grandiose, is to act as a bulwark of democracy, to be the eyes and ears of the public. To watch councils and governments and law courts and report what they do in our name. Reporting may entertain. But more than anything it informs.

That journalism is important, that journalists can make a difference has rarely been better expressed than by one of the founders of the *Independent* newspaper, Stephen Glover, writing in the *Spectator*. The occasion was the death of a young British journalist who had gone out to make his name in Iraq at the end of the war in 2003, when the country seemed to be descending into lawlessness: 'What is one to say about Richard Wild, the 24-year-old inexperienced journalist shot in the head in Baghdad? He was by all reports clever, decent, brave, good. It seems such a waste. What would he have produced had he not been murdered? A few seconds of footage which might, or might not, have flickered on our television screens, and then been forgotten. And yet this is all that journalism ever is. No single article or programme ever makes much difference. It is their cumulative effect which counts. The hundred or so reports which Richard Wild never filed would have made a difference. They were worth taking a risk for. It may be no comfort to his parents and friends, but this young man died in a noble cause.'

So yes, journalism can change things. The bulletins filed by the BBC television reporter Michael Buerk were credited with alerting the world to the great Ethiopian famine of 1984. The *Sunday Times* won a celebrated victory for press freedom in 1979 when it won the right to publish its detailed investigation into the effects of the drug Thalidomide, which had caused deformities in unborn babies.

The benefits of a questioning, free press are clear. Some journalists go so far as to suggest that the constant position of the reporter must be one of scepticism. According to the mythology of the *Sunday Times*, its celebrated editor Harry Evans – the man who fought the British courts over the Thalidomide story – suggested that any aspiring journalist interviewing a politician should do so while thinking: 'Why is this bastard lying to me?'

Some critics find that attitude too cynical. They worry that reporting politics is becoming more attractive than being a politician, to the detriment of political debate in this country. Others are attracted to that level of scepticism, whether applied to politicians, businessmen or the police. Few have used scepticism to greater effect than the television interviewer Jeremy Paxman, whose sneering interrogative style, accompanied by a raised eyebrow to indicate profound disbelief, has unsettled the most experienced politicians. The *Today* programme presenter John Humphrys has developed such a reputation for acute questioning that the Prime Minister, Tony Blair, started to appear on the programme only if the more emollient James Naughtie was handling the interview.

You see that disdain too in the attitudes of the *Channel 4 News* presenter Jon Snow, who thought students were letting the side down when he spoke at the *Daily Telegraph* conference in 2002. Where was the journalistic passion? What had happened to the idea that journalism could expose wrong and make the world a better place? 'I'm surprised that people aren't more angry. I suppose times are mellow, and everyone's drunk and stoned. But we were drunk and stoned – and we were angry, too.'

Perhaps apathy goes in cycles, in which case we are due some anger soon. Perhaps a new, more polemical generation will desert the show business circles of the 3am Girls in favour of rattling the gates at Westminster. As for drunk and stoned, perhaps we had better address that now.

There have, traditionally, been two things said with certainty about journalists, particularly British ones. They are drunks and they are unreliable.

Let's deal with the drinking first. I arrived in Fleet Street in 1981 in what turned out to be the dying days of real excess. There were still journalists who kept whisky bottles in their bottom drawers and found it difficult to start any story without a stiffener. A colleague at the *Daily Telegraph* routinely dictated his stories to the news desk secretary because he was too drunk to focus on the typewriter keys.

The natural place to spend time between assignments was the pub. The obvious place to go to lunch was the pub. The first call after work was the pub. At the start of the 1980s, those few journalists who chose to spend their spare time at the gym were suspected of homosexuality. By the end of the 1980s, there were lots of them. The serious drinking was almost over.

It's not that there is no more drunkenness – only recently a top reporter moved from one paper to its deadly rival and, in a drunken stupor, rang the phone number of his old employer to dictate an exclusive story. Naturally, even as his new news desk wondered where he had got to, his old paper printed his story with a bigger by-line than he had ever got when he worked there. But the drinking is now under control. Like the rest of industry, newspaper managements expect sobriety from their workforces during working hours.

So what about the unreliability? Here is an American journalist called Larry King – not the Larry King who presents the CNN television interview show – writing on an American website devoted to journalism edited by Paul E. Schindler Jnr, himself a former newspaperman: 'Those of us forced to read the London papers sometimes speculate about which is greater: the average British hack's sloth, mendacity, ignorance, obsequiousness, capacity for drink, or aversion to paying for that drink. Smart money tends to split between the latter two.'

It is not an altogether original observation. Samuel Johnson came to a similar conclusion almost 250 years earlier. News gathering, said Dr Johnson, 'required neither genius nor knowledge, neither industry nor sprightliness; but contempt of shame and indifference to truth are absolutely necessary. He who by a long familiarity with infamy has obtained these qualities, may confidently tell today what he intends to contradict to-morrow; he may affirm fearlessly what he knows that he shall be obliged to recant . . .'

And here is the actress Zoë Wanamaker, quoted in 2003, when she was starring at the National Theatre in a stage adaptation of another brilliant film comedy about newspapers, *His Girl Friday*: 'Journalists are people I have a very healthy disrespect for.'

There are journalists who resent this reputation, but most tend to wear it almost happily, as a mark of twisted pride. After all, it is not your business as a journalist to be liked – or not to be liked once you have got the story you were looking for, at any rate. The attitude was caught nicely by the British poet Humbert Wolfe, in 1930:

> You cannot hope to bribe or twist
> (thank God!) the British journalist.
> But, seeing what the man will do
> unbribed, there's no occasion to.

So journalists grew up aware that it was not their role in life to be liked or trusted. That is why many were shocked by the results of an opinion poll conducted by the pollsters YouGov in 2003 and published in the *Daily Telegraph*.

The orthodox view was that journalists were generally held in low esteem, somewhere around the bottom with other bad people such as estate agents and politicians. Remarkably, the YouGov poll discovered a crucial difference in the way broadsheet and tabloid journalists were regarded.

The survey of around 2,000 people discovered that broadcast journalists were among the most trusted of all members of the population. Reporters from ITV, *Channel 4 News* and the BBC were ranked closely together, sandwiched between local police officers on the beat and head teachers in state schools. They were ahead of vicars and priests.

Journalists on broadsheet papers – the *Telegraph, Times, Guardian, Independent* and so on – also came out of the survey pretty well. Sixty-five per cent of those members of the public who were questioned said they trusted these journalists to tell the truth a great deal or a fair amount. This put them only one place behind judges and actually ahead of senior officials in the United Nations (the survey was conducted in the spring of 2003, when the United Nations was constantly in the news over weapons inspections in Iraq). Right behind broadsheet journalists and safely in the top half of the table came local newspaper journalists. They had the trust of 60 per cent of those questioned.

Journalists on the mid-market papers such as the *Mail* and the *Express* were in the bottom half of the table, just ahead of trade union leaders. Thirty-six per cent trusted them. But it wasn't until the pollsters asked about journalists on the 'red top' tabloid papers – the *Sun*, the *Mirror*, the *Star*, the *News of the World* and so on – that the traditional view emerged. They came bottom – below car dealers and estate agents – and were trusted by only 14 per cent of those who took part in the poll.

Who came top? Doctors, of course, pretty much as we suggested at the start of this chapter. They were trusted to tell the truth either a great deal or a fair amount by 93 per cent of those questioned. Schoolteachers came second, registering 88 per cent trust. There wasn't a question about investment bankers. But as we said at the start, they have all the joy that money brings.

You might think that this unexpected perception of trustworthiness would have brought great pleasure to all broadsheet journalists. They were being allowed, after all, to walk tall among members of the public. Strangely, they seemed rather miffed, having long come to terms with pariah status.

Naturally, other stereotypes persist: the journalist is still the man in the dirty raincoat standing on the doorstep. She's the neurotic woman who makes a declaration of friendship as she conducts the interview, then plunges in the knife when she writes up the piece. Well, all right, I could put names to both those descriptions immediately. Several names, in fact. But most journalists would recognize neither themselves nor their colleagues in that description.

For this is an industry with a remarkably varied range of work. We'll talk about getting in and getting on later, but the way in for most people is local newspapers or what is known as the trade press – specialist publications covering different areas of industry or special interest. Just as local newspapers can be very local – the *Dawlish Gazette*, for example, sells 2,400 copies each week in Devon – so trade magazines can be very specialist: *Electric Railway Society Journal* goes out six times a year to some 400 readers who are interested in electric railways around the world. They are, says the magazine, mostly male. There is, you will find, a seemingly endless supply of esoteric titles tailor-made for the headline competition on *Have I Got News for You?*

Some journalists see these titles as stepping-stones to something bigger, others gain career satisfaction from working in one place. Just as many GPs take professional pleasure in making a lifetime's contribution to one neighbourhood, so there are journalists who are proud of the knowledge they accumulate and the service they bring to a place – often the area they grew up in – over many years. Editors of these titles become key figures in the local community. They tend to believe their papers uphold standards of accuracy beyond those of the national press. In the same way, there are journalists who remain on specialist magazines and build up such knowledge of the industry or interest group they cover that they become prominent figures within it. Naturally, there are others who see their first titles only as a means to an end – a chance to learn the business before moving on.

This is why it is difficult to generalize about journalists: how do you begin to compare a piece by a highly knowledgeable writer for a specialist publication such as *Jane's Defence Weekly* with a story from a news reporter on a local weekly? What has the cub reporter who goes out to interview elderly couples about their golden wedding anniversary got in common with the hip magazine writer reviewing the rap singer Eminem? Here is a man who has spent his working life reporting on the local council for his local paper – no one knows more about the Town Hall than he – and here is a woman who has worked for five different papers before the age of thirty-five and covered everything from music to health. The only obvious thing that connects them is that someone is paying them to write articles and stories.

We haven't even begun to address the thousands of journalists who move out of papers, magazines, radio and television and into other businesses to handle information or public relations briefs. There are journalists in companies, charities, councils and government departments. Some of these have become very powerful, none more so than Alastair Campbell, the man credited with masterminding the media strategy that brought Tony Blair to power. Mr Campbell was never elected, but he became one of the most important men in government with his iron grip on 10 Downing Street and on Mr Blair's ministers. Nevertheless, if you were thinking of a word to describe him, you'd probably have to call him a journalist.

Because they are all over the place, it is hard to be precise about the number of journalists working in Britain. The Newspaper Society, the umbrella organization for local and regional papers, says its members employ about 8,000 journalists, a number that has been declining since the 1980s. Newspapers are businesses. The fewer employees they have, the more money you can make. That means papers look increasingly to using staff journalists only for the words they can't get from news or other syndication agencies. Big national newspapers such as the *Telegraph* or *Mail* each employ more than 500 journalists across their weekday and Sunday titles. A good guide to the number of journalists around – however much their job title disguises their trade – comes from the National Union of Journalists. It reckons to have a third of all journalists in Britain and Ireland as union members. There are 34,000 in the NUJ, which puts the journalistic population of the British Isles at just over 100,000.

What are the qualities you need to become one of their number? The National Council for the Training of Journalists is clear: 'An interest in current affairs at all levels; a lively interest in people, places and events; an ability to write in a style which is easy to understand; good spelling, grammar and punctuation.'

The NCTJ also suggests 'an appreciation of the part a local newspaper plays in the community; a willingness to accept irregular hours; an ability to work under pressure to meet deadlines; determination and persistence'.

It would be hard to quarrel with any of that, though many now manage to get into the industry without much interest in the role of local newspapers. The qualities required were famously put in snappier form by the late Nicholas Tomalin, a *Sunday Times* foreign correspondent: 'The only qualities essential for real success in journalism are rat-like cunning, a plausible manner and a little literary ability.' Mr Tomalin was killed on the Golan Heights in 1973 when a heat-seeking Syrian missile hit his car during the Yom Kippur War. He was forty-two.

Sometimes, as you come across a cynical old reporter or watch a bunch of middle-aged sub-editors at work, you have to ask whether they ever had energy, enthusiasm and interest. The kindest thing to say is that they are transformed at the hint of a big story. Then the life returns and they are young again. Nothing rejuvenates like a front-page splash.

At least they have the defence that they have been kicked about a bit over the years. There's no such excuse for newcomers. I have been amazed when, from time to time, some young reporter has suggested it would be difficult to pursue an inquiry into the evening because he or she has a date. This is no way to get on.

No, to make an impression, you have to go in with the idea that you are signing over your life for a while. The paper, radio station or news agency is going to own you.

If it is a parish council meeting that keeps you at work for the evening, you have to convince yourself that it is the most important parish council meeting in the world. If you are not prepared to slog round that rough estate late at night to find the missing witness, a rival paper may be. If the news desk asks you to start going through all the Smiths in the phone book in an attempt to turn up the Smith whose son has just been killed in a road crash in France, you'd better get phoning.

Of course there are skills you may never have to use again: some reporters pride themselves on their ability to prise pictures of dead children from their grieving relatives, others feel physically sick at the thought of even knocking on the door. As a news editor, I don't mind a reporter who recognizes the latter symptom, as long as he or she pulls off the former skill. There are news reporters who are brilliant at finding facts and incompetent at writing stories. They make great reporters, as long as someone helps put those facts in order. Sports reporters do not bother themselves, by and large, with the details of Cabinet reshuffles. Feature writers, however, should always bother themselves with the business of facts.

But what all have in common is a sense of the day-to-day demands of the publication for which they work. A newspaper or magazine or news organization is dealing with perishable goods: a story filed after the deadline is worthless.

So, just as mothers adapt to the feeding demands of children, journalists find that their working rhythms begin to adjust to the requirements of the title. By 3 p.m. on an evening paper you know that only a very good new story is going to make it into that night's edition. Sunday journalists who relax into long lunches on Tuesdays become nervous by Saturday morning, because if they haven't a story by then, they are not going to get one. Daily journalists work with half an eye constantly on the clock.

It is more than five years since I worked on a Sunday paper, but sixteen years on the *Sunday Times*, *Sunday Telegraph* and *Independent on Sunday* have ensured that a peculiar twitchiness still sets in around teatime on Friday, which is pretty much when it becomes clear whether a week's edition is going to work. Several months after moving off a news desk, I still reached urgently for any ringing phone, even in the houses of friends.

This is all very good for the working cause, but does not always do a lot for personal relations. The paper becomes the third figure in a marriage, the one with the power to have you walk out of family parties, cancel dinner arrangements and break promises. Some papers make it a sackable offence for reporters to come to work without a passport although it is more likely they will be travelling in Britain. It's not that you want to do it, you explain, it's that you've got to: 'I'm really sorry, but I have to get up to Manchester tonight.' 'I'll try to get back for the birthday party, but this is a huge story.' 'The Prime Minister's resigned. There's no way I am going to get away to meet your parents.'

And somewhere, someone else clears up a little of the mess and you get on with being a journalist, bringing the world the news, fulfilling your responsibilities to the paper and – you can't admit this to anyone – having such an interesting and exciting time *that you would do it even if they didn't pay you.*

2

Getting in

When you are trying to get into journalism, you come hard up against the syndrome Joseph Heller identified in his celebrated novel, *Catch 22*. Newspapers employ people with experience; how do you get experience without being employed?

You quickly notice something else: there is a big queue. You are going to have to push your way to the front. Things aren't as bad as in the theatre, where more actors get to spend their time 'resting' than ever make a name for themselves, but the last twenty years have seen a remarkable rise in the numbers who decide they want to be journalists.

Think of this queue as good practice for how you are going to have to behave once you are in. If you can't face the pushiness required; if you are worried about the sales pitch you have to make to get through the door; if you are too thin-skinned to take the pain of rejection, perhaps journalism isn't for you. As a news reporter, you learn to knock again when a door is slammed in your face. You may as well start learning now.

This ambition to get into journalism is often only a vague aspiration. There are veterans of school magazines and university newspapers who have mapped out a career path that will see them editing the *Guardian* by the time they are forty (and you realize, with a sick feeling, that one of them is going to achieve it); but there are also people who don't feel ready to grow up and who reckon journalism looks better – in the words of its critics – than working for a living (twenty years after I started, my father would still ask when I thought I might get a grown-up job); and there are those who are desperate for some sort of fame and who think journalism might be a way to find it (what they really want is to be talent-spotted to present a Saturday morning children's television show, but someone has told them that journalism would be a good place to start).

There are two traditional ways to get in: you find a job on a newspaper or a magazine or with a news agency. Or you get writing and hope that someone agrees to print your piece and to pay you for it.

Before you try either of these, you may decide you want to build up your CV with a course in journalism. This is still a 'may' because journalists do not need journalism degrees in the way that doctors need medical degrees. Indeed, once you are in, you soon find that no one cares much at all about qualifications. But you might find that a degree equips you not only to find a job more quickly, but also to fit in faster when you do.

If you get the right teaching, a college or university course might also encourage you to think a little more about what you want to get out of journalism. You can find everything from correspondence courses to block-release sessions to a three-year undergraduate degree or a one-year postgraduate qualification. We will talk more about these courses – and the difference between journalism and media studies courses – later in this chapter.

Before we do, let us look at your chances of finding a job.

It all used to be so simple. You joined a local newspaper and learned how to be a reporter. Like apprentices of old, you were indentured to the paper and paid very little. They taught you shorthand and how to write a story and a little bit of law and, after two or three years, you took an exam set by the NCTJ and, if you passed, qualified as a senior reporter, at which point you got paid a little more. Then you worked your way up to a bigger local newspaper, and either made a career for yourself in provincial journalism or jumped to a national title in Glasgow or Manchester or London.

By and large, the only journalists who broke this rule were graduates whose brainpower and analytical power were believed to be so great that they were taken straight on to national newspapers as leader writers. Ah, you might say – I know we all did – I bet they would be no good at writing a hard-news story. Indeed they wouldn't. But then they will probably never have to because they will be so busy writing important think pieces about international politics.

Only twenty-five years ago, most reporters in the newspaper industry were school leavers rather than university graduates. There are still journalists around – some in very senior positions – who started off as newsroom messenger boys when they were sixteen. Journalism was always a democratic business: there were openings for scholars who could write erudite leaders on Church doctrine and openings for wide boys whose English wasn't too good but who could charm the bereaved into parting with family photographs.

You might imagine that the graduates moved towards the broadsheets – the so-called quality newspapers – and the school leavers to the pop papers. There would be some truth in this – just as, in the provinces, the morning papers tended to be keener to recruit graduates than were their evening siblings. But, like all generalizations, it is only half true. It's true, for instance, that Rebekah Wade of the *Sun* and Richard Wallace of the *Mirror* came into journalism as school leavers (although Ms Wade refers to attending the Sorbonne in her *Who's Who* entry, this does not appear to have been for a degree course); it's true that Martin Newland, editor of the *Daily Telegraph*, went to Goldsmiths' College, London, and that Alan Rusbridger of the *Guardian* went to Cambridge. But Peter Hill, the editor of the *Daily Express* (and previously of the *Star*), went as a mature student to Manchester University; Simon Kelner, the editor of the *Independent*, was at Preston Poly, now the University of

Central Lancashire. Paul Dacre, editor of the *Daily Mail*, went to Leeds University, Robert Thomson, editor of *The Times*, became a cadet reporter in Australia – we call them cub reporters in Britain – after leaving school.

While we are on generalizations, you may also have heard that the difference between tabloid and broadsheet journalists is that tabloid journalists dress better. That one's true.

These days, most of the trainees entering the business are graduates. This is partly because more people go to university and partly because the industry has become so popular that it has no problem attracting graduates. In the words of the Newspaper Society, the body that represents the regional press, newspapers are 'flooded with inquiries from thousands of would-be journalists'. The basic requirement is five GCSEs, one of which must be English, although the majority of applications now come from graduates. Some are recruited directly by regional or local newspapers and carry out basic training under the terms of an in-house training contract. Others are recruited from one-year full-time vocational post A-level courses held in colleges accredited by the NCTJ. Some of these courses are specifically tailored for graduates.

Some regional groups offer training programmes. Otherwise it may be down to individual papers to recruit trainees as and when they need them. Go to the internet sites of the regional groups – companies such as Johnston Press, Trinity Mirror and Newsquest – to get the most up-to-date information.

Some national newspaper groups have also started their own training schemes. the *Daily Telegraph* has recently moved specifically to recruit trainee sub-editors, because that is where it thought it was short of good, young applicants. *The Times* and the *Financial Times* each takes on two or three trainees a year, the former sending its recruits on the postgraduate course at City University, London. The *Sun* and the *News of the World* also use City University for what they proudly call their 'scholarship' scheme. Trinity Mirror takes graduate trainees not only for its regional titles but also for the *Mirror* itself. As you can imagine, there is extremely tough competition for places and no guarantee of continued employment, but if you take your chances these are short cuts to the heart of the national newspaper industry. The national news agency, the Press Association, and the worldwide agency, Reuters, also take trainees for a variety of posts. How many they take, and in what roles, varies from year to year. Again, you can track what is going on from their websites. The editor of the *Spectator*, *Daily Telegraph* columnist, sometime television panellist and Conservative MP Boris Johnson, started life as a trainee with *The Times*. He has written himself that things did not always go well. Then he talked his way into a news feature-writing job on the *Daily Telegraph*, after which he never looked back.

It is also possible to leap straight on to a national paper – or at least to get shift work – as a diary reporter. These are the men and women who write those paragraphs of social news, gleaned from assiduous attendance at parties, from bits of gossip and stories that tend not to stand up well enough to make the news pages. Your chances here, I must warn you, are greatly increased by Knowing Someone, an important aspect of journalism.

The rise of the graduate, like so many of the developments in journalism, has had good and bad effects. On the one hand it guarantees a stream of entrants who have been educated to a higher standard, which might be thought to have a beneficial effect on standards within the industry. On the other hand, degrees do not noticeably confer higher moral qualities. Nor do they guarantee any obvious journalistic benefits, such as an ability to spell. As far as local newspapers are concerned, graduates tend to have no more perceptible skills than school leavers, but are rather harder to mould. They get ideas above their station, don't do what they are told and are ambitious only to get in and get up. There is a danger that reporters become culturally detached from the world they report and develop ambitions to write beyond the straightforward, clear, simple, objective reportage that should be the foundation of all newspaper reporting.

This can be unhelpful for local papers, which traditionally operate on the principle that many of those who join come from the local area and from among the people whose lives they will report. They have always expected many trainees to move on when they have qualified, while working on the basis that some won't. It is hard to acquire local knowledge if you intend to stay no longer than a couple of years.

Having said that, I can think of several people who started their working lives around the same time as I did, on the *Star*, Sheffield, and who remain there. They have stayed because they like the area, they like the paper and they like the work. There are journalists who think that national newspapers are the be all and end all. There are others who believe that the nationals have lower standards of accuracy, rely on sensationalism and do little that is good. I can think of at least two former colleagues who, having done well on Fleet Street, decided to return to the provinces because they felt that local journalism was more worthwhile.

In 2003, the *Western Daily Press* feature writer George Frew caught perfectly the joy of provincial paper journalism in an article he wrote after being diagnosed with terminal lung cancer at the age of forty-eight. The news came, he explained, just as he felt professionally fulfilled: 'We liked Bristol. We liked where we lived and the city itself. I was working with some of the best journalists of my career on a wonderful newspaper.'

So it's the local paper for you and, along with several thousand other would-be journalists, you apply for a job as a trainee. Whether you are writing to a local weekly or to a national daily, to the BBC or, indeed, to one of the college or university courses in journalism, certain rules apply. You must find a way to convey two things: not only that you have the skills to do the job but that you really have the desire.

Everyone applying – or everyone who is going to get beyond the first stage – will claim energy, enthusiasm, determination, a willingness to work under pressure and an interest in people. You might go half a step further in demonstrating in your letter that you can write English – you would be amazed how many applicants show

24

no interest in spelling or in apostrophes – and that you have done some elementary research.

It helps, for instance, to discover the name of the editor and the correct title of his or her newspaper. This isn't difficult. Go to your local reference library and get down a copy of *Benn's Media* or *Willings Press Guide* (the first sells at £395 for a four-volume set and the second at £325 for a three-volume set, which is why you may prefer to go to the reference library rather than buy either for yourself). These books cover the world, with whole volumes dedicated to the British media. You will find all local papers listed, together with details of circulation. The name of the editor could be out of date: check it by phone. Knowing the right name might not get you the job, but starting your letter with the greeting 'Dear Sir/Madam' will guarantee that you don't.

Gerald Isaaman, the long-serving editor of the *Hampstead and Highgate Gazette* – the 'Ham and High' – had a reputation for being particularly hot on the spelling of his name. They say they want to make a name in journalism, he would explain; they can start by learning mine.

He was right. Any letter from a would-be journalist addressed to me as 'Miss' or 'Ms' Fletcher goes straight in the bin. If they are not bright enough to establish whether this Kim is male or female, they can go and work somewhere else, if anyone else will have them. It is very easy to kill off an applicant you have not met, a person who is no more than a name at the end of an incompetent letter. All employers are looking for reasons to weed that list of letters to a shortlist for interview. Don't make it easy to weed yours.

Then read through the letter and cut out every word that does not need to be there. Once you are earning a living as a feature writer you can play around with adjectives. This letter should be as succinct as a front-page news story and ideally as compelling, without a spelling mistake or literal – a literal is where you write liretal when you mean literal – in sight.

So far so good, you haven't given any reason to be crossed off. Now what are you going to say to push yourself into the interview category? The most helpful thing would be some demonstration of a commitment to journalism, probably written as part of the CV to which your letter directs the reader.

The school magazine will do for a start. Student journalism is better still. If you have ever had letters published in your local paper – surely you kept the cuttings – so much the better. They suggest a long-standing interest in journalism. Stories, as in short stories, are not a good idea: editors are looking for reporters, not would-be novelists.

You might also impress if you have made a start on other skills. I don't think my having enrolled at night classes in shorthand clinched my own application – I certainly hadn't learned much shorthand – but it did suggest I was serious about the business. So did the fact that I had learned to touchtype. You don't have to: most journalists still don't. But why not, when it is so easy to learn?

I suspect, however, that I clinched it at the *Star*, in Sheffield, in 1978 with my answer to one question: 'And if you could work on any national paper, which one would it be?'

'The *Daily Mail*.'

'The *Daily Mail*! That's a change. We get so many graduates coming in and saying: Oh, the *Guardian*. The *Guardian*, the *Guardian*, the bloody *Guardian*.' It was true that I admired the *Mail*. I guess I also had a sneaking feeling that my interviewers would too.

Try it by all means, and do remember that not all middle-aged newspaper executives share the reading enthusiasms of student journalists. Mind you, if it's true that all students want to be 3am Girls now, you may find that every student is already going in naming the *Mirror* rather than the *Guardian*.

If you really know the paper to which you are applying – perhaps you live in the area – it is better on the whole to avoid criticism. In films, the young maverick who produces a brilliant critique of the product and explains how he will make it better is immediately taken on by the company boss. In real life, he is shown the door. You may feel your local paper is failing in all kinds of ways, but the editor will not be eager to hear this. Wait until you have got your job, at which time you will be able to pass your views off as the endearing enthusiasm and impatience of youth.

If you do know the area, however, there is everything to be gained by playing the local card and explaining your lifelong ambition to take part in the essential guarding of democracy that is the function of our press. Editors, like everyone else in journalism, rise to flattery.

But still the rejection letter drops through the door? Then send off more applications.

You are invited to an interview? Then start preparing now. This is vital, whether you are applying to a newspaper or to a college course. Why walk into an editor's office knowing nothing about her newspaper when you can go in with the circulation, that day's splash and the name of the star columnist in your head? Will a university lecturer be upset to discover you have done some reading about his faculty? Or cross that you haven't? Why wait for an editor to raise the decline in his city's local industry when you can raise it first? You may have no interest at all in football, but if the local team is one of the reasons the paper sells, you should at least know its name.

None of this information is hard to find. You should be cagey about 'facts' on the internet, but information posted by local councils ought to be reliable, at least about such things as size of population. You will find too that even the smallest papers publish websites. They don't give you a feel for the paper in the way that hard copies do, but they do tell you what kind of news is happening locally and whether the paper is running campaigns.

Look through back issues in the online archive for a tell-tale 'council climbdown' or a local employer 'bowing to pressure'. These are the fruits of a local newspaper campaign. Get to know the story. Now you have something to congratulate the editor about.

Journalists need to know that someone has read their pieces. Editors love to hear that someone has read their paper. I promise you, as long as you show even the slightest sign of knowing what you are talking about, they will be very pleased.

If these don't sound obvious things to do, you need to give a lot more thought to your preparation. If they *are* obvious, you will be amazed to find that you are in the minority. Most applicants fail to do their homework. When I applied as a graduate for a job in Leeds twenty-five years ago, I was struck by the surprise on my interviewer's face when I discussed the evening paper I had bought at the station the night before. Clearly, few of his interviewees had thought to do the same.

Things don't seem to have changed. Twenty years later, when I went as deputy editor of the *Sunday Telegraph* to speak to journalism students at Sheffield University, I began by asking how many had seen the paper the day before. Only a handful had. They all knew someone from the *Sunday Telegraph* was coming. Pure curiosity, never mind journalistic expedience, should have sent them to the paper beforehand. Last year, at the University of East London, a few more claimed to have read my current paper, the *Daily Telegraph*. Naturally, they were the ones I treated with greater respect. I didn't expect them to like the *Daily Telegraph*, still less to buy it every day. I did expect them to have looked at it that day.

Only a foolish or hopelessly under-prepared journalist would go to interview the head of a local factory or the leader of the council without doing a little research. You must do the same when you are going for a job interview.

There is one other important consideration when writing a letter of application. Do you go for broke by writing in a way that stands out from all the others? I write 'go for broke' because it may be a work of such genius that the recipient can't help reaching for the phone and calling you in for interview that very minute. On the other hand – and I fear the odds are on this – it may stand out for all the wrong reasons and so irritate the editor, course director or training officer that it goes straight into the file marked 'Rejects'. Either that, or it is passed around with a snigger.

I remember, shortly before I left the *Star*, a senior colleague in Sheffield handing me a letter from a young woman eager to join the paper. Most of it was given over to the thoughts of her cat, Tiddles, who had learned of his mistress's ambitions to become a journalist.

'"A journalist!" said Tiddles, looking up from his toy mouse. "That sounds interesting."

'"I think it will be," I said, pouring him a special saucer of cream.

'"And will we be able to read your stories on the front page?" asked Tiddles.

'"Oh yes, if that nice man from the *Star* gives me the job. Then I'll come home wearing a trench coat and a trilby hat," I said, tickling the soft fur under his chin.'

I asked the assistant editor how he had replied. 'I wrote telling her we had no vacancies,' he said. 'But I put a PS at the end: please give my love to Tiddles.' Case proved, you'd think. Except that I was working on Fleet Street soon after I had left the *Star* and was astonished to watch Tiddles' mistress walk straight into a job on a paper that was just starting up, the *Mail on Sunday*.

It would be wrong to leave the subject of first jobs without discussing one other area that has proved fruitful over the years for many journalists, most of them women. We have looked at applying specifically for reporters' jobs. But a great many of our most successful journalists have come into the industry by way of work as editorial assistants, personal assistants or secretaries.

Typically, recruits to this area of the business are more likely to gravitate to feature writing or reviewing; arts and books pages, women's pages, food and drink pages. But there is no reason why they should stay there. This is the route followed by, among others, Veronica Wadley, editor of the *Evening Standard*, and Rebekah Wade, editor of the *Sun*. Before she became an international cooking star, Nigella Lawson was a successful newspaper columnist. She found her foothold not as a reporter, but as an assistant on the books pages of the *Sunday Times*.

The advantage of this way in is that you apply directly to a national newspaper or magazine. If it is your ambition to work for *Vogue*, then you feel you are on your way if you can land a job as an editorial assistant at Condé Nast. The disadvantage is that there is no career structure or training, no guarantee that you will effect your escape to actual writing, and very little money in it unless you do.

To be working in London as an editorial assistant on a glossy magazine as a 22-year-old graduate may seem the most glamorous thing in the world, especially if your contemporaries have disappeared to work as cub reporters in the provinces. To be working as an editorial assistant three or four years later, when those same contemporaries are hitting town to find work as by-lined writers on Fleet Street papers, is not.

Anyway, it would be remiss not to point out that this kind of job is not often advertised. Some more cynical readers may already have read at least one of the names above with some tightening of the lips. Are these jobs, by any chance, more a case of who you know than what you know?

Well, yes. What Nigella Lawson has achieved since, she has achieved through her own talent. But whether Andrew Neil, then editor of the *Sunday Times*, would have offered her a job on his paper if she had not been a daughter of the then Chancellor of the Exchequer is another matter.

There are so many sons and daughters of journalists in the business that no one raises an eyebrow when another turns up. When familiar names turned up at the *Telegraph* Max Hastings, who came himself from journalistic stock, saw no point in denying that there was nepotism at work. He has suggested there may be a genetic predisposition to journalism. After all, no one expresses surprise when doctors follow doctors, lawyers lawyers and actors actors. A third-generation member of the Deedes family – the grandfather is W. F. Deedes, once again reporting for the *Daily Telegraph*, the father is Jeremy, a former managing director, acting editor and chief executive of the *Daily Telegraph* – is making his way at the newspaper. The grandson of John Junor, a celebrated editor of the *Sunday Express*, is racing up the ladder at the *Daily Telegraph*.

As a first-generation journalist myself, I arrived in London with all the chippiness that the North can bestow and watched aghast as a succession of privately educated children of journalistic or political or famous stock discovered opportunities that seemed to be denied to their contemporaries.

But I also realized that because they had in effect been brought up in the industry, the journalistic offspring arrived with a good idea of what was wanted. As for the others, they came aglow with the confidence that the trade requires. Totally misplaced confidence, in some cases, for it also became clear that the ones who weren't good didn't last. Finally, they might have got a head-start, but they couldn't stop pushy, talented outsiders from muscling in.

So if you haven't got a name, or you weren't bred to it, or you are not absolutely outstanding or tremendously attractive and you really don't know anyone already working there, you may have problems finding that job as an editorial assistant at Condé Nast. But think about whether you have got some skill – a knowledge of books, an insight into fashion – that you could parlay into an assistant's job on the relevant newspaper desk. Then it is a case of seizing the chance to do some writing.

Perhaps, however, you are not looking for a job. Or not yet, anyway. You have a proper job elsewhere, which it would be foolish to leave. Or you want to make your way with all the freedom of that gun for hire, the freelance journalist. Here is the second route into journalism; you write a piece and some newspaper or magazine editor likes it enough to print it.

In this field, it is possible to make a little experience go a long way fast. Someone on the end of a phone telling me that she has never done any journalism but would like to write a piece fills me with gloom. Someone introducing herself by detailing two or three pieces she's had published gets my attention.

But what could those pieces be? Let's divide journalism roughly in two: news and features. In effect you can divide all journalism into one or other group, whatever section of the paper is involved. A family of four dying in a road accident is a news story. It might include some words from the father of the dead mother. But a set-

piece interview with the father – 'My brilliant daughter, our gor-
geous grandchildren' – is a feature, even if it appears on the news
pages. Manchester United sack Sir Alex Ferguson is a news story;
'My Fury: Sir Alex Speaks' is a feature. The manufacturing firm
making 500 staff redundant is news; the interview with the chief
executive, in which he explains the future of the company, is a
feature.

There are further divisions you can make, but however you
describe comment pieces and analysis pieces and opinionated columns, it is hard to slot them into any category other than features.

There are many journalists who make a good living from freelance reporting. But unless you are remarkably well plugged-in to
some newsworthy area of life, you are unlikely to succeed without
a great deal of experience. You may find work as a member of a
news agency, but that is not very different from being taken on by
a newspaper.

With the exception of foreign reporting, which we shall come to
shortly, feature writing rather than hard news is the more likely
opening. There are – as there always are – exceptions.

You may lead a strangely eventful life, in which buses crash in
front of you, fires break out down your street and political assassi-
nations disturb the customers at your local café. There may also be
occasions on which, through some unexpected freak of fortune, a
big story falls into your lap. A family friend has advance warning
of a factory closure; you find yourself in the middle of a riot; you
learn that a local councillor is also pushing drugs.

In situations such as these, you should get hold of a news desk
and try to sell a story. We shall see how in later chapters. But it is
more likely that your early pieces will build on the news rather than
break it. To give an example, you have local knowledge of the
tensions that have led to an outbreak of summer rioting. The
national newspapers will send teams to pick over the causes. You
could act as the fixer who tells them where to go and sorts out
interviews. You might not see your by-line on the piece at the end

of it, but you have got yourself a fee from the paper and an 'in' with the news desk.

Or you are, perhaps through some family connection, unusually well placed to secure an interview with a figure in the news who otherwise refuses to talk to the press. Provided you deliver what you promise, you begin to build yourself a reputation. At the very least, someone at the paper or magazine will listen when you ring with another idea; at best, the paper may think of you when allocating a story that has come up in features conference.

Finally, now that papers are as interested in features as in news, there are all kinds of ways to turn your life and your interests into stories. You may be the first person to tell the national newspaper features desk of a new craze sweeping the clubs, the first to spot the latest summer toy that has been taken up by the nation's children, the first to explain the appeal of the new drug that is terrifying the parents of teenagers.

There are people at every newspaper whose job it is to spot trends and commission pieces on them. They can't do it without people like you. How many times have you read a feature in a newspaper or magazine and thought: 'But I've known about that for months. Fancy them only getting round to it now'? There are stories under our noses, if we only think to look.

That's not the kind of journalism I want to do, you say. It may not be. But it is the kind of journalism that gets you into a newspaper, makes you contacts, gives you experience and gives you the chance – perhaps – to move into the kind you do.

And then there is foreign reporting. Once, national newspapers kept large staffs abroad. Now they don't. Once they have staffed Washington, New York, Paris, Moscow, Beijing, Brussels, Jerusalem and Johannesburg – pretty much in that pecking order – there is nothing left in the budget for expensive foreign bureaux. Indeed, the middle-market and popular papers are unlikely to have a staff reporter anywhere other than America. There are several reasons for this: readers are felt to be less interested in foreign news; a reporter abroad is conspicuously expensive when nothing much seems to be happening; in days of limited editorial budgets, don't you get more impact by spending on features and entertainment at home? Foreign news agencies cover the gaps and, with 24-hour television channels covering the globe, you can catch up pretty quickly.

For all other cities – at least until they can get their own 'fireman' out there to run big stories – newspapers rely on 'stringers' or local freelances. Stringers usually get small retainer payments and more when they file; freelances earn when they file.

Foreign desks are always looking for more names in cities abroad, on the arrangement that they pay only for the stories that they ask for. If a big story breaks, the more hands on it the better. Once you persuade a desk that you are capable of writing a story, your name will go into the contacts book. The day they can't reach their own stringer or the regular freelance, you are in. In the meantime, you look for the kind of features that will interest magazines and specialist titles.

The real trick, which is very hard to pull off, is to move to an area that is going to become big news. Get it right, and you will find yourself in the middle of a very big story. Misjudge your global politics and you could spend months in a country no one cares about. During the fall of communism in Eastern Europe in the 1980s, a number of young reporters managed to do just that, establishing themselves in cities such as Prague, Warsaw and Buda-pest when nothing much seemed to be happening. They built their careers on the reputations they established when the communist regimes began to fall apart.

A decade later, another generation made a name for itself – and secured full-time jobs as a result – from being in the Balkans in time to report the start of the break-up of Yugoslavia. It didn't matter that newspapers sent staff reporters out to cover the war as it developed: the reporters on the spot were needed for the local knowledge they had built up.

Last year, a group of young journalists – some with experience, some without – took a similar gamble in moving to Baghdad after the fall of the regime of Saddam Hussein. They went to establish an English language newspaper, to be at the centre of a big, big story. For Richard Wild, who had a little experience of working in the ITN office in London, it turned into a tragic gamble. He was murdered within days of his arrival.

And so, finally, we come to journalism courses. Old sweats sneer at these. What can you learn that you do not learn on the job, they ask. How can you teach journalism other than in the newsroom?

A salesman from the *Daily Telegraph* classified advertising team came to see me to confide that he was about to resign, having decided he wanted to become a reporter rather than work on the commercial side of newspapers. Would it help, he asked, to put his savings into a year's course at a London college?

It was, unfortunately, impossible to give a sure answer. He would finish his year knowing some shorthand and how to construct a news story, and he would probably have the basic qualification from the NCTJ, but he should not expect those skills to guarantee admission to some editorial floor. If he did not have basic journalistic instincts, no amount of course work would get him a job. If he had good instincts he might well get in somewhere without doing such a course. On the other hand, a course would make him more confident and might encourage potential employers to believe he was serious in his ambition.

He was talking about a commercial course at a private college, but the question is further complicated by the many university courses that have sprung up offering graduate degrees and post-graduate diplomas in journalism. These have made many of the old sweats crosser still. Certainly they have a point in questioning whether some of the practical disciplines taught on such courses require the academic brainpower traditionally associated with universities. Shorthand?

First, we should distinguish between media studies courses and journalism courses. Unfortunately, when they apply, many students do not. Courses in media studies concentrate on the theory of media communication – how and why messages are conveyed and the effect that they have – rather than the practice of journalism. Students are encouraged to analyse the communication of news and culture. They may be taught to dissect a news story: they are not taught to write one.

There is a good deal of analysis on journalism courses too, but it comes with practical tuition. Thirty years ago, postgraduate courses at University College, Cardiff, and City University, London, gave journalism university status, something it had long had in the United States. Until then, journalism had been taught on the job and within centres set up by newspaper groups or under the auspices of the NCTJ.

Teachers on those first university courses encouraged their students to question practices and to bring new aspirations into the business. But while they asked them to lift their sights, they also taught them the basics required by the newspaper industry: shorthand, a knowledge of the law and of local government, the construction of a story.

The graduates of those courses did not go straight on to national newspapers. They did find it easier to find work around the provinces and, when their contemporaries were joining weekly papers, typically found places at evening and morning titles.

Now those early courses run alongside many others, most of them designed for undergraduates rather than postgraduates. The popularity of journalism means that some of these courses have been able to ask for high academic standards from large numbers of applicants, though they have discovered that academic excellence may not be the best way of recruiting good future journalists.

It is highly unlikely that newspapers, radio and television will ever demand degrees in journalism in the way that firms of accountants now look for accountancy degrees. But they will look on a journalism degree as evidence of a real ambition to work in the business. They will also know that trainees come to them with many of the rudiments of the trade in place and will thus be quick to work unsupervised.

You may decide that for these reasons, you should think seriously either about a journalism degree or a course at a college of further education. It won't turn you into the finished product and you should not be surprised if your first employers continue to regard you as a trainee. But it may give you the confidence that will make a difference in a newsroom. It will also expand your horizons and encourage ambitions in a way that should be good not only for you but for journalism as a whole.

Loved and Loathed:
Insiders' Tips of Dos and Don'ts I

John Carlin, foreign correspondent, the *Observer*

Dos
- File on time
- Be attentive in your copy to spelling, grammar and obvious facts, e.g. dates
- Be respectful and engaged with colleagues, especially superiors
- Be respectful and engaged with everybody you interview
- Write accurately, but also with enthusiasm.

Don'ts
- Turn in messy late copy
- Complain all the time (as opposed to very infrequently indeed) to people on the desk about the way they edit your copy
- Demonstrate your insecurity by continually coming across as clever know-all, in your copy and with colleagues
- Be too flip
- Be too pompous

Charlie Catchpole, television critic, *Daily Express* and *Daily Star*

Dos
- Show enthusiasm (real or feigned) for even the most seemingly mundane and boring assignments. These can be the ones that unexpectedly produce a result.
- Show willingness to work long hours, uncomplainingly, if asked. At some point, the time spent standing on doorsteps will be more than compensated for by long periods idled away doing nothing
- Dress smartly. This may seem unimportant, but I am amazed how many young reporters turn up to the office these days looking as though they've been sleeping rough. You never know where you are going to be sent, and people are more likely to open up to a journalist in a suit and tie than someone in jeans and T-shirt
- Show persistence, whether having to shout through the letterbox of a door that has been slammed in your face, or when you are being threatened
- Show willingness to help 'rivals' on other papers with quotes, etc., if – through no fault of their own – they are trailing behind on the story. But only, repeat only, once you have filed your story to your own paper. Such kindness is sure to be reciprocated

Don'ts
- Demonstrate ignorance of the subject in hand. There is no excuse for not reading the cuttings and having even a superficial knowledge of the story
- Behave rudely. However much you may disapprove of someone you are talking to, don't let it show
- Show disregard for basic accuracy; spelling, dates, facts and figures, etc. Never leave it up to the subs to check. Why should they? They are under enormous pressure

- Show off/put yourself centre stage in the story. Always remember, you are not the story
- Fail to pay your way in the pub afterwards with your thirsty colleagues

Mark Henderson, science correspondent, *The Times*

Dos
- Brim with ideas – they are the backbone of good journalism. Not everything will make a story, but the more thoughts you generate, the more chance you have that one will work out
- Acquire a reputation for making difficult projects work. This involves persistence, lateral thinking and refusing to take no for an answer. The task you're set by an executive might look impossible, but there's usually a way to pull it off. Even if you can't deliver everything on the news editor's wish list, getting close will make you trusted
- Write clear, clean and concise copy. Don't just assume the subs will tighten up your loose copy – if your intros never need rewriting and your English is error-free, it will be noticed and appreciated
- Write fast, to deadline, and file your copy as early as you can. If you're known for being able to turn around a breaking story in twenty minutes before deadline, you'll become invaluable. Many news pages have to be typeset early in the day, and have to be filled: if you can write something by 3, do it – you may find it gets a much better show than it would later in the day
- Co-operate with your picture and graphics desks. The right illustration can make all the difference between a story leading page three and ending up in the news in brief column

Don'ts
- Miss the story. The reporter who can't spot a story's best angle more often than not is living on borrowed time

- Be precious about your copy. You might feel attached to your purple prose, but don't be surprised or angry if it gets chopped to pieces by the newsdesk or subs. Equally, avoid using jargon and over-long words and phrases
- Be inaccurate. An honest mistake is not the end of the world, but serial inaccuracy and a cavalier attitude to facts will get you into trouble very fast
- Let people down, or lack enthusiasm. If you say you will do something, do it and do it properly. If you can't be relied on you will soon be found out. Equally, if the newsdesk don't think you're going to give a story your best shot, they won't give it to you. A reporter who isn't 'up for it' is not going to last long
- Tread on your colleagues' toes. Make sure you check before you write something that impinges on a colleague's patch, particularly if that person is senior and/or touchy. Be a team player, and give credit to colleagues who've helped you on a piece – don't be a 'by-line bandit'

3

Getting on

We have already discussed the fierce competition to get into journalism. Once you're in, you realize that this is nothing compared with what goes on *inside* the business.

Of course, everyone is familiar with the notion that journalism is competitive. British journalists thrive on the belief that they work in the toughest newspaper market in the world. It may even be true. In the United States, many big titles such as the *New York Times* have near monopolies. Here, with a rivalry that amounts to real enmity in every sector of the market, no paper can be complacent about its readership. Everyone naturally thinks of that competition in terms of rivalries between publications. The *Sun* and the *Mirror* each work hard to do down the other; the *Daily Mail* keeps the *Daily Express* under constant surveillance; the first thing the editor of the *Daily Telegraph* does – before even looking at his circulation figure – is check that his paper is better than *The Times*.

Naturally, such competition has its comical moments. In 1987, for example, the British press discovered that Spanish villagers planned to throw a donkey from a stone tower as part of unfathomable Iberian celebration. The first day's coverage, naturally enough, was the revelation that this horrible act was about to be committed, and an enterprising reporter improved the emotional charge of his story by giving the donkey a name: Blackie. The second day's coverage became the fight to save the animal. The *Star* was first to get to Blackie with enough money to persuade his owners that he should be spared. That left the *Sun* and the *Mirror* with a big problem. How could they show that Blackie was safe, when he was in the protective custody of their deadly rival? There was only one solution: find another donkey and buy that one too. By the end of the week all the papers had a Blackie the Donkey. The readers of each could feel they had played a part in this act of compassion.

These are rivalries that burn deep into the consciousness of the journalists who work on these titles, though it is true that these allegiances change as often as a journalist changes papers. A writer for the *Sun* whose main motivation is to produce better stories than anything the *Mirror* publishes may happily sign for the *Mirror* the following week.

And throughout the world of magazines, a weekly or monthly battle goes on for supremacy in each given sector. It is not enough to be *a* magazine in the construction, marketing or beauty sector. It is all-important to be *the* magazine. These editors conduct postmortem conferences not only on their own magazines, but also on all the rivals. Is their fashion better? Why didn't we get this interview? How did they uncover that news story?

So yes, most of those stories of reporters trying to do down their rivals are true. In the days before mobile phones, reporters really did disable public call-boxes to prevent rivals using them; they do pay witnesses to go on holiday to get them out of the way of other papers; of course the man from the *Mail* reads hotel messages that are meant for the woman from the *Express*. The crucial thing is not only to get the big story, not even to get it before anyone else, but to get it without anyone else getting it at all.

That is the dynamic that drives so many dramas about journalism. But there is another force at play, with which you may be less familiar. This is the rivalry that takes place within titles. In journalism you are in constant competition not only with rivals on other newspapers, but also with every colleague on your own paper. Could I have written that story as well as she did? Why didn't the news desk put me on that one? That's never a front-page story!

Writing journalists – let's forget sub-editors and commissioning editors for a moment – know that each edition of the paper, the magazine, the programme, reveals not only who has been working on what, but also whether that work is any good.

Each day is a fight to establish your worth. You show me someone who doesn't mind whether his story makes the paper and I will show you a liar. Find me a reporter who doesn't care how big her by-line is, and I shall hand in my press card.

It doesn't matter how small the magazine or how big the national paper. Publications have a peculiarly public and transparent hierarchy. The world does not know who teaches the best lessons, who has made the most money in a bank, which lawyers are on the up. But everyone in and outside journalism can tell who has written the front-page story, the biggest feature or the most important interview. Star feature writers get their pictures all over the page as a matter of routine. News reporters must discover the missing Lord Lucan, bring down a government or come under gunfire to achieve the same glory.

There are, amazingly, hundreds of reporters working away for news agencies or for magazines such as the *Economist* – which is too self-important to believe in by-lines – who do not get to see their names in print. There are others who find professional satisfaction in producing a well-argued leader article or in commissioning, editing and improving the work of others. But most journalists never recover from seeing their by-line in a newspaper and become addicted to the pursuit of more.

Talk to my old friend at the *Sunday Telegraph*, who was so unhappy at seeing his pieces cut that he had to leave journalism to become a historical biographer. In his days on the paper, he would take galley proofs of his stories home from the pub on a Friday night, tracing his name with his finger and reading the intro over and over to whichever luckless minicab driver happened to be working the Isle of Dogs around throwing-out time. He never seemed to notice whether they spoke English.

Or, if, around 10 in the morning, you take the London Underground Jubilee Line to Docklands, home of the *Mirror*, the *Indepen-*

dent and the *Telegraph,* keep an eye open for the journalists on their way to work. They will be the ones watching other passengers reading their papers, dying a little inside as the readers turn straight past the article over which they sweated the day before.

As a friend of mine in the newsroom at the *Sunday Times* once confided, waiting for the first edition to come up on a Saturday night was like Christmas: 'Seeing your story in the paper is like finding your present under the tree. Sometimes you're on the front page and it's a really big, exciting present. Sometimes your story is inside the paper and it's just an ordinary sort of present. And sometimes your story hasn't made the paper at all, which is like seeing a present under the Christmas tree for everyone except you.'

This doesn't mean that newspaper offices are unpleasant places. On the contrary, I cannot imagine where you could find a greater spirit of comradeship and shared purpose, where rivalries are so quickly put aside over a drink. Colleagues go to great lengths to help one another. They offer advice and share contacts. They fetch and carry facts for colleagues writing against the clock.

But in reading every edition, they evaluate the work of those same colleagues; analysing strengths and weaknesses; giving public praise and keeping criticism to themselves; working out where they stand in the pecking order, and how they can move further along it.

Is there a quick way up? There is, but there are no signposts.

Piers Morgan was made editor of the *News of the World* when he was just twenty-eight. You can imagine the envy that must have promoted among all those more experienced journalists who had imagined they were in with a chance of the job themselves. He had worked for a South London newspaper and as editor of the Bizarre pop column on the *Sun.* The story is that he was working late-night subbing shifts on the *Sun* when the editor, Kelvin MacKenzie, spotted him. Mr MacKenzie was looking for someone to run Bizarre and asked Mr Morgan what he knew about show business: 'Not much.' 'Great,' said Mr MacKenzie. 'You'd be perfect.'

He *was* perfect, creating a name for himself as a friend of the stars, a claim he established by having his picture taken with them at every opportunity. It was enough to get him noticed as an editor for the *News of the World*. Two years later he moved to the *Mirror*.

Rebekah Wade became editor of the *News of the World* when she was thirty-one and of the *Sun* when she was thirty-four. In ten years she had risen from being a junior editorial assistant to sitting in the editor's chair. Like Piers Morgan, she had some indefinable quality – a little ruthlessness, a real tabloid flair – that suggested to Rupert Murdoch she would make a good editor. Tabloid flair? It is an ability to look over a day's news events and select the ones that will surprise or entertain a popular readership. They are not usually the world's most important stories: they are, to your audience, the most interesting. Tabloid flair lies in clever story selection and lively presentation, irresistible headlines and seductive layout.

Those two are exceptions, but they are not so exceptional that they prove any rule. In this respect, journalism is like show business. Some are plucked from nowhere to become stars, some rise slowly, many do not rise at all.

If you look at the 2,300 local and regional, paid for and free newspapers and the 8,000 magazines that are published in Britain, you might expect to find some kind of natural progression. Surely, newspaper journalists will move from a weekly to an evening and perhaps on to a bigger evening or a regional title. Then they might make a leap for Fleet Street, which despite the great move out to Docklands and other anonymous office blocks, remains the generic name for the national papers that once clustered along a half-mile stretch of the famous street. In the parallel world of magazines, they will see a way from title to title, trading up for bigger circulation or better reputation or more interesting subject matter.

Indeed, these are the routes followed by most journalists, unless they decide they will never like a job more than the one they have got, or they fall in love with the town where they work, or in love with someone who won't leave the town where they work. Or, of course, they have no ambition, which in journalism is a much more serious failing than having no talent.

At any stage in this progression you might land an outrageous stroke of fortune that lifts you up and pushes you up the path. A national newspaper editor takes such a shine to your work that he offers you a job. Working as a freelance, you uncover a story of such significance that you can demand a staff job from the paper you approach. Or – most likely of these three – your father is such a popular figure on Fleet Street that one of his friends is eager to take you on.

It's still more likely that, if you want to make the move from provincial to national papers, you will have to take a chance, resign your job and move to London in the hope of picking up the regular newsroom shift work that might lead to a job. When you work a news shift, you hire yourself out as a reporter, at the beck and call of the news desk that has hired you for the day or the night. You may find you have signed on for eight hours of boredom. You may find yourself in the middle of the biggest story of the day. This is where those who work for the London weekly titles can take a short cut. If Fleet Street is a long way from the *Newcastle Journal*, it is practically next door to the *Hackney Gazette*. Some local journalists don't have to pack up the day job to sign on for shifts with the nationals.

Others work hard to build up unofficial contacts with national news desks while working in the provinces. Proceed with care, for you may find that the news editor, the chief sub or even the editor has built up a lucrative sideline in selling tips on local breaking stories – the address everyone is looking for, the quote from the murdered man's mother – to the nationals. They are far enough up the ladder to get away with selling on some of the fruits of their colleagues' labours. If you deal only in the stories you are working on yourself, and pass on only information that is going to appear first in your paper, you should be all right, but be discreet. When the time comes to look for shifts, your contacts on the nationals ought to feel that they owe you one.

I used to think that, once I had enough front-page splashes in my cuttings file at the *Star*, Sheffield, I would be welcomed into the newsrooms of the nationals. Then I discovered that everyone trying to find a way out of the provinces had cuttings like mine. Suddenly those big Sheffield blazes, missing kiddies and South Yorkshire murders didn't seem so newsworthy.

Nor, on the other hand, did I find myself out of my depth on my first shifts for the *Daily Mail*. It was then that I really realized the merit of learning the business at a good provincial paper.

It has become something of a cliché on Fleet Street that we tell bright young journalists who have broken into the paper from nowhere that they should get themselves off to the provinces to pick up some experience. This conversation typically takes place when they begin to think that they know it all and deserve a staff job. Some listen, dutifully retreat to the provinces and are never heard of again. Some don't, refuse to let go and are practically our bosses within six months. Is it good advice?

Let's tot up the balance sheet. Firstly, follow the advice and you will get a good grounding in all forms of journalism. You will learn reporting skills that you will never forget – not just the basics such as story construction, but how to work information out of people, what makes them tick and why there are different perspectives. With that kind of grounding, you can walk into any national newspaper newsroom and be confident that you can do the job.

The best newsrooms harness youthful passion to middle-aged experience. But they expect even the passionate young to know enough about the business not to need babysitting. A few years in the provinces gives you enough. When a big story breaks, your experience kicks in. Given time, you *can* pick up this kind of experience on a national paper. But national newspapers are not renowned for giving time.

And secondly, just because you have joined a paper in a small provincial town, there is no reason to lose touch. You can continue to develop the contacts you have made on a national title by offering stories or help to visiting reporters working on your patch. You may also find you are in a more fruitful area for finding your own stories: most stories on national papers are given out by news desks. On local papers you are expected to come up with more of your own, which may offer greater job satisfaction. There are also greater opportunities to try different skills: you may be offered 'colour writing' – that's when you can start putting your own adjectives into stories – or sports reporting, or even your own column.

Thirdly, it is tremendous fun. An unknown town or city is waiting for you to make your mark on it. You are young and will find a gang of other young people working with you. The journalists I know who went through the provinces talk as happily of those days as they do of their university life. They carry with them a shared experience of the comedies, dramas and tragedies of human life, of magistrates' courts and council chambers. They think still of the surprising warmth of kindly people on forbidding council estates, the pomposity of local officialdom and the pleasure of heavy drinking when you are young enough to shrug off the hangover.

Finally, you are not going away for ever. Those contemporaries who have got themselves to London and claim to be making a living from occasional shifts and diary work may patronize you when you sign on for low pay on a provincial paper in an unfashionable town. But three years later, many will still be looking for a breakthrough – 'I do a bit here and there' – when you return with the experience that will find you a job.

What about the case against? If you are managing to make a living out of pieces for national papers and magazines, why take a step back to work in the provinces? You have clawed your way in, the security man has stopped asking to see your pass as you walk in, they will have to give you a job soon.

You are making a name. You are new and young, the qualities every editor likes to look for. You are 'hot'. They like you. But if you disappear from view, some other young hopeful will take your place and, in time, the job that was earmarked for you. And if things don't work out where you are, you are beginning to make contacts on other papers. Anyway, you like it in London, it's where the action is and your friends live. Why go to Hull to learn the ghastly business of 'clearing the mantelpiece' – running off with all the pictures a grieving mother possesses of the teenage daughter who has just been killed in a road accident – when you know all you want to do is become a political editor? Three years? That sounds an eternity.

Yes, it is easy to see that learning the business at a provincial paper will lead to a basic level of proficiency. But won't it also lead to newspaper cliché and an unwillingness to question? Would it not be the enemy of innovation and imagination? In any case, what is all this about needing to learn the skills? Have I not just graduated from one of the most highly rated university journalism courses in the country? I feel perfectly competent to walk into any national newspaper. Indeed, when I see some of the raw copy that the old pros turn in, and the mediocre pieces that are printed, I think they need me and my ideas more than I need them.

Once you set it out like this, I can see why those who have managed to find their way into a national paper, on however impermanent a basis, are reluctant to leave of their own accord. But I also know which group I would trust immediately to set to work and produce something of publishable quality.

In describing the good impression you must strive to make, I have suggested that the only man or woman whose eye you are working to catch is the editor. On smaller newspapers and magazines, this is likely to be so. If you are applying for a job on a provincial newspaper, it is the editor to whom you should write.

But if you are trying to have a piece published, you may do better to approach other figures. For while it is true that, on some publications, no word is printed without first being read and approved by the editor, most newspapers – and a few magazines – are too big for the editor to read everything in advance, to know all the freelance journalists providing stories or, indeed, to be aware of all the copy that is coming in. In terms of power, newspaper and magazine staff take their place in a pyramid at the top of which sits the editor. Every now and then, someone tries to operate a new magazine on a collective basis, but there are so many unresolved arguments that they hardly ever get the thing printed on time.

This pyramid may be very big in the case of a paper such as the

Daily Mail, or quite small for a magazine such as the *New Statesman*. But whatever the size of the pyramid, the editor will be there at the top. All power ultimately vests with him or her: he or she is responsible both to the owner or publisher and also in law for what ultimately appears in print.

Not all editors necessarily behave in the same way. Their styles vary, but almost all come to develop something of the tyrant about them. In the days when I worked news shifts one summer at the *Daily Mail*, the then editor, David English, was a far-off deity. We lowly reporters glimpsed him in the evening on the back bench – the production section that puts the paper together – sitting in a chair with the inscription EDITOR on the back. When I was a news reporter at the *Sunday Times*, the then editor, Frank Giles, was a remote figure whom it was possible to see only by appointment. Older hands compared him with his predecessor Harry Evans, who had been a regular presence in the newsroom, encouraging reporters in their work. By the time I edited the *Independent on Sunday* there was such a collegiate culture at the paper that it was impossible to stop the most junior freelance from wandering into the editor's office.

That had more to do with the culture of the *Independent on Sunday* than with changing times. The *Guardian* maintains a practice of allowing into editorial conference all who wish to attend: the *Mail* would regard such democracy with horror. Naturally, the more senior you become on a paper, the more frequently you meet the editor. If senior executives become blasé about editorial conference, reporters attending it for the first time do not.

Journalism differs from other businesses because the editor is not only the most senior figure short of the proprietor but is visible on the shop floor, taking decisions every publishing day. In any newsroom, there is a heightening of tension, an increase in drama, at the sight of the editor on the floor, reading pages, questioning stories.

The editor, naturally, has a deputy, who runs the paper when the editor is away and dreams of running it full-time. Sadly, deputies

rarely inherit the title. They work instead as the editor's chief
enforcer, seeing that the editor's demands are carried out.

Then comes a series of important figures on the paper who may
have specific responsibilities for different sections or who may
interfere where they like, depending on the instructions they have
from the editor. You can spot them by their rather non-specific
titles: they will be called executive, or associate, or assistant editor.

Next comes a bank of less senior editors, each with responsibility
for a section of the paper: the news editor, the features editor, the
sports editor, the business editor, the arts editor, the chief sub-editor
and any others that the editor may wish to create. Again, depending
on the size of the publication, they may have deputies or other
underlings to help with the smooth running of those sections.

It is tempting to say that the bottom of the pyramid is made up
of the writers, but it's not entirely true. In general, feature writers
are imagined to have unique talents that gain them a commensur-
ately higher status. Specialist reporters – the health correspondent,
education correspondent and so on – are also regarded as being a
cut above. It is general news reporters who like to think of themselves as the poor bloody infantry, supporting the entire pyramid.
In fact, the more successful ones enjoy good status within the paper
and some – though this tends to be more true of feature writers and
columnists – enjoy such privileged status that they report directly
to the editor.

The newspaper structure is not very different from departmental
government. In this analogy, the section heads are Secretaries of
State. The editor is Prime Minister. Morning conference, which
discusses the content of each day's or week's magazine or newspaper, is the Cabinet meeting.

The more you see of the system, however, the more it actually
appears to function as a medieval monarchy. The section heads are
barons fighting for preferment – more space in the paper, more
staff, more money – and the editor is an absolute monarch whose
every whim must be accommodated.

Nothing galvanizes a newspaper staff faster than an 'editor's must'. This is a story that, come what may, needs to be followed and written and published in a form that satisfies the editor. Sometimes editor's musts are very specific requests. Occasionally they are inferred from oblique conversations, with the result that the entire energies of the paper are directed at something in which the editor does not recall even expressing an interest.

Thus, when an editor looks through his paper and muses to morning conference: 'Are we doing enough about crime?', the news and features desk will return to the editorial floor to drum up coverage of compelling crimes. The editor may look through the pages and suggest there are too many pictures of old people: from that day on, no one over forty will get his picture in the paper, until Bob Hope dies, when it is impossible to avoid it.

So where, as an outsider offering stories or seeking work, do you sit in this hierarchy? The medieval court analogy holds good. If you are brought in at the request of the editor, then whichever section head has charge of you will treat you with respect. No courtier extends his career by insulting protégés of the King. If you are half-way competent, you will be pronounced a genius. If you are utterly useless, it will take some months for anyone to pluck up the courage to say so. There are many writers around whose talent remains an utter mystery, but because they managed to cling to the rock on the basis of an initial introduction, it is far too late to prise them off.

If, as is more likely, you come in to write a news story, or a feature, or to help with a special supplement, then you must work to impress the baron or baroness in whose territory you find yourself. Every executive on a newspaper likes to discover talent: junior ones to show that they are ready to climb the ladder further, senior ones to demonstrate why they have risen so far already.

If you are lucky, you will find commissioning editors with the confidence to judge your ideas and your work for themselves. But it is common to have to wait for them to elicit the views of someone further up the chain, both before commissioning the idea and deciding whether the written version is any good.

You should work very hard to make a friend of this point of contact – the news editor, features editor or whoever. If your first story works out, he or she will be happy to take another. A piece may even 'work out' without being published, for there are all kinds of reasons why many excellent stories and articles never make it into print. The point is to show that you can deliver what you promise, that your story stands up to the claims you made and that you meet the required deadline.

With a piece under your belt, you are on your way. If you can get two or three ideas taken up, you are well placed to get a call the next time they are looking for someone to develop an idea that has come up at the paper or magazine. Ideally, this relationship flourishes when it develops into a mixture of ideas you put up and things they want you to do. In this way you become a regular contributor, a relationship you can seal by suggesting you come into the office to meet for a talk.

Be warned that there are niceties to be observed. If you look as if you might be a success, your first contact is going to want the credit for introducing you. So when you have an idea that you know would be right for another section of the paper, put it first to your contact, explaining that it doesn't sound quite his or her thing, but would it be all right to suggest it to the sports editor?

They know they may in time have to pass you on to someone higher up the chain, but they would like a little acknowledgement of their role in your discovery. Never ever forget the people who give you your first breaks. It's not only bad manners, it is also very stupid. If they never achieve anything else in journalism, they have done you a service. If they continue to rise then they will remember an absence of respect.

There is a third party who can intrude on this beautiful relationship, either ending it for ever or fanning it into passion. Yes, it's the editor. You are unlikely ever to have met. But now you have produced a piece of work that has caught his or her attention. Is this your big break – the moment that means you have a future on the paper? Or is it disaster, the guarantee that no one will commission you again?

Let's look first at how it can go wrong: your piece is written, the commissioning editor is pleased with it and you wait confidently for it to appear. The last you heard, it was all set to run, so you rush to the newsagent the following day to buy the paper. You turn over the pages, looking for the features. As one page turns into another, you realize that you are into the health features. Your heart sinks, for you know that your piece had nothing to do with health. A feeling in the pit of your stomach tells you that your piece is not there, but, against all the odds, you hold on to the hope that it will miraculously appear before the business pages start. It doesn't.

You ring the commissioning editor to ask if there has been a problem. You have a last hope that all is well and the piece is merely waiting another day. But he tells you something you don't want to hear. He tells you the truth. The piece was in the page ready to run, until the editor read a proof of the page and decided to drop it. Now you have only one hope: that the piece was dropped purely because the editor liked another more, or felt the balance of the page was wrong. If it was dropped – the cruel newspaper word is 'spiked'[1] – because the editor did not like it, this is a black mark against you.

It could be worse. Let's imagine that you skipped off to the newsagent's and, just as you dreamed last night, found your piece sitting proudly in a prominent place on the features page. You are, you feel, on your way. But even as you are ringing round your friends to inquire if they have seen the fine piece in that morning's *Telegraph*, an inquest is taking place at the newspaper offices. The editor is going through the paper and stops at your page: 'Was

---

[1] The term 'spiked' is derived from the days before copy was handled on computers. When stories were written on paper, rejected stories were stuck on metal spikes. Reporters who sense that the stories they are working on are unlikely to get in the paper still say that they are 'writing for the spike'.

there any point to this piece? It was badly written and full of clichés. And who is the writer?'

The writer is a journalist who only ever got his name in the paper once, for the editor's criticism has kissed goodbye to your career before it started. The editor doesn't need to say you are not good enough to write for his or her paper: the entire editorial conference has just made a mental note of that fact. To commission you again the section editor would have to explain to the editor that you really can cut it. Are you worth that investment?

But let us look on the brighter side – at that wonderful moment when the editor reads your piece and announces that he likes it. When things go badly, the executives at conference are quick to decide you are not to be encouraged. When things go well, they are just as eager to use you again.

You are not yet, in Mafia terms, a 'made man', but you are someone it is safe to put up as a writer. If the editor asks who you are, you can now be safely described as the writer who wrote that very good piece on the features page the other day.

I saw this in action most graphically at the *Daily Mail*, when, in one of my freelance periods over the last twenty-five years, I was asked to write a piece about a dancer in a West End show. She was a black girl who, the show business editor discovered, had been adopted by a white couple in Surrey. Now she was on the way to stardom.

The piece appeared and was given a remarkable amount of space. The following day the commissioning editor was on the phone. The piece, it turned out, had brilliantly synthesized David English's obsessions about race, the Home Counties middle classes and musicals. '*The editor loved it. The editor loved it.* We must meet. How are you fixed for lunch? Now what are you going to write for us next?'

But even the luckiest break doesn't guarantee you a job for life. If you are going to make a career of journalism, there are some basic requirements. In an ideal world – one in which the reader could have faith in all that appeared in print – the key attributes would be honesty, accuracy and energy. That is the origin of the orders once written on the walls of newsrooms: 'Make it fast, make it first and make it accurate.'

But because it isn't an ideal world, the biggest laugh comes with the extra order, pencilled at the end: 'Make it up.'

It's a good gag, but it isn't fair. Let's be idealistic. The more journalism strives for truth, the better journalism gets. In actual fact, most reporters on all papers work hard to get to what they believe to be the truth. They joke about inventing quotes but labour to get real ones. Naturally, to obtain the necessary element of excitement, they write the story as hard as it can be written, using get-out clauses as a kind of insurance policy. Once you know the code, you can't help noticing these.

Phrases such as 'set to' – as in 'Government set to imprison rich people' – are a giveaway that the action in question may never happen. A paragraph that ends 'it was claimed last night' puts the bald statement that went before it in perspective. Claimed by whom? By a sane, responsible observer? Or by a local nutter, out to attract attention? 'Plans' – as in 'council plans to ban private cars' represent an aspiration that may never come to fruition. The council was planning to do it, the reporter explains, when asked why the story failed to come true. Then it decided not to proceed. 'It was true when I wrote it.' Then there is 'up to' – as in 'up to 1 million people' – a gratifyingly vague amount that implies many while possibly referring only to a few.

Unfortunately, stories that have been pushed as far as they can go by reporters get pushed further still by sub-editors. The qualifying clauses disappear. Stories that involve shades of grey become black and white. The language of headlines – short, direct, enticing – adds to the confusion.

So let us make a stand now for honesty and accuracy. They are not only good for journalism, they are also in your own interest. A freelance who makes mistakes is a freelance who doesn't work again. Get these things wrong on a local paper and you will have the news editor on your back. Keep getting them wrong and you

will get a bad reputation. You might also find that the person you
have written about is waiting in reception to meet you. He will be
big. He will be tough. And he won't be bringing you a bunch of
flowers.

Next, couple accuracy and honesty with energy. News desks give
out the best stories to the reporters they believe will best execute
them. There is everything to gain by earning a reputation as the
reporter who knocks on twenty doors when others try three. You
will soon find that people who will not speak on the phone open
up when they are confronted on the doorstep. You spoke to ten
neighbours who saw nothing? What if the eleventh watched the
whole thing?

I can't help remembering my interview with the news editor and
his deputy at the *Sunday Mirror*, when I was new to London and
applying for shifts. They were an infamous pair, much pilloried in
Private Eye as a pair of outrageous cowboys.

'So you are coming to freelance?' He spoke in a parody of a hard-
bitten news editor, crossed with a theatrical agent. 'Then you are
going to clean up. If you are fast, and accurate, and you can come
up with stories, Fleet Street is your oyster.'

I wasn't sure what I could come up with, but when you have just
packed in a secure job to take your chances, they were the words
you wanted to hear. I never did get a piece in the *Sunday Mirror*,
but his words gave me the push I needed. They also implied that
this could indeed be a big adventure. There are some other good
journalistic words to go with accuracy and honesty and energy:
'confidence', 'conviction', even 'cockiness'. Try them on. You may
not think they fit immediately, but walk around as if they do. Soon
they will feel quite comfortable.

4

How to sell a story

Some freelance writers who perform for newspapers are so successful that they need never lift the phone to petition for work. These
are the journalists who have escaped the petty concerns that plague
the rest of us: ideas, deadlines, and where the next cheque is coming
from.

Typically, their comfortable status has been conferred by a couple
of novels or by the celebrity that television brings. They are stars, so
they sit at home and allow themselves to be persuaded by supplicant commissioning editors that it would be fun to fly to the
Caribbean to produce a travel piece, to be chauffeured to that sell-
out Rolling Stones concert to write a colourful review, or to sit in
the best seat in Cardiff to produce an alternative view of the Cup
Final.

They can afford to be too grand to discuss money, preferring to
leave it to their agent, the one they took on when they got their first
book deal. That way, the agent gets the reputation for grasping rude-
ness and the writer remains warm, friendly and accommodating.

Not so accommodating that they can be bossed around, of course.
These writers have the confidence to explain that it would be
impossible to produce the piece in time for the next day's paper.
They have, they point out, many other calls on their time. They
imply that papers and magazines need them more than they need
papers and magazines – an implication that commissioning editors
appear to accept.

No one likes to stop to ask whether this is true, for the newspaper industry works on the basis that there are some writers who sell copies. And if, as occasionally happens, the piece the talent writes is not up to the usual standards, no one suggests that the talent reworks it until it is right. If an article does not work out first time, it is more likely to be the commissioning editor who takes the blame. So these writers get their money anyway, even if the article is never published.

Journalistic celebrities receive letters of praise and van-loads of flowers from the editor, and other blandishments that make life swell. They are indulged in the way that Hollywood studios indulge successful actors. Commissioning editors tell them that they are loved and that they are wonderful. This is called looking after 'the talent'.

You, sadly, are not one of these people.

If you wait for the phone to ring you will wait for ever. You must get out of your chair and beg, flatter or bully for every piece of work. You have to hustle commissioning editors with story ideas, bounce back from every rejection and believe that you are going to get your work published. And in case they ever do ring back, you need to make sure that you never take more than nine seconds to answer the phone. Otherwise they will be ringing someone else.

All right, all right, we are being a little melodramatic. This is not quite the world of *Pop Idol*. But you have no real experience and you know no one at the paper. If you did, you would be ringing him or her every day seeking an introduction. Fortunately, things are not quite as bleak as they seem. There is one commodity that every newspaper and magazine needs, one that makes or breaks commissioning editors. The commodity is ideas.

The most common question that journalists are asked by those outside the business is: how do you decide what you are going to write about? Readers are often puzzled about the process that sees one group of seemingly random events, commentaries and inter-views make it into print over another group. Where do stories come from? Is there, on any day, one obvious lot of words to put in a paper? How do you find these magical newspaper orchards, where articles hang from journalism bushes, waiting to be plucked?

Sometimes, of course, the process is easy to follow. When terrorists fly hijacked planes into tall buildings, no one sits around wondering what to fill the news and comment pages with. Over on sport, the calendar of events dictates basic coverage. If it's May, it must be the Cup Final. The City pages are driven by the quarterly round of company reports. But beyond the obvious, there is a constant demand for ideas.

The 'burn rate' is high. Newspapers and magazines eat up ideas. Naturally, many never make it into print. Some fall instantly: old, obvious, stupid, pointless, impractical, untrue, done by the *Mail* last week. Others collapse under the weight of the first phone call made to check them out. Many get as far as being written before anyone realizes that they are not actually very interesting. There are journalists who dream ideas as naturally as they breathe: a simple news story stimulates notions for three more. There are others who haven't a thought in their heads until it is planted by a news editor. To make your first break, you must be one of the first group.

We've talked before about the pyramid-like quality of a newspaper hierarchy. That shape is mirrored in the flow of ideas, with many more swimming around the bottom than ever make it to the top. It is the job of each section editor to work out how to fill his or her section. Some ideas for doing so may be directed from above – there will always be things that the editor wants to see in the paper – but most will be the responsibility of the section editor.

Not all of these will be obvious. Take news, for example. Each day there is a long list of news stories that we might call public property: political announcements, crimes, accidents, disasters. They are reported by the national news agency, the Press Association. Every radio and television station, every newspaper hears about them at the same time.

But there are also stories that may be exclusive. A specialist reporter has discovered through his contacts an important scientific development, a prominent politician has decided to reveal something to a particular paper, a clever bit of thinking has worked out that a seemingly small event could have much bigger implications.

You can see immediately that it is the second group of stories that will do more for the reputation of the paper and those who work on it.

The future of a section editor depends on the list of ideas he or she can come up with to please the next level up. A Sunday newspaper news editor may lock his news reporters in a room for half an hour until each has come up with three ideas for that week's paper. Features editors return in panic from morning conference after being told that every idea put forward is rubbish. They have half an hour to come up with new ones. A monthly magazine editor is about to sign off a feature spread when he opens a fortnightly magazine and finds it's just been written better.

You have to become the journalist who can help out, the one who has a grip on youth culture, the writer who has recognized the latest craze before any of the papers have woken up to it, the outsider who spots things of interest that escape the notice of editors who spend their lives in offices.

The biggest mistake made by would-be writers is to offer pieces to papers that they have clearly never read. Pick up the *Daily Telegraph* and find me an article on its comment pages that is longer than 1,000 words. You can't. So why do so many otherwise intelligent people send in 2,500-word opinion pieces believing they will be published?

Or why do you imagine, in the week that the *Guardian* has published a feature on the Rolling Stones growing into their sixties, that it will now commission your thoughts on ageing rock stars? Yet many inexperienced writers do, all the time.

What does the editor of the *Mirror*, who runs a weekly film review column written by a highly paid writer, want with your thoughts on the latest *Matrix*?

'Didn't you see our piece yesterday on the new generation of mobile phones?'

'Er, no. I don't get the *Mail* every day, actually.'

'Then come back and try to sell us a story when you do.'

The next error is to imagine that papers care what a young student writer with no specific experience thinks about the war in Iraq, or America's place within the world, or the problems of global warming. They don't, unless the piece is so well written or so striking that it demands publication. Every now and then – let's say once in 500 manuscripts – such a piece drops on a desk and gets noticed. Otherwise it goes in the bin.

As always, there is an exception to this rule, but you won't want to hear it. If you are the son of a politician and you are writing a view that is not your dad's, or your mother is a big name in show business and you have embarked on a career in modelling, then commissioning editors will be happy to give your piece a second look.

In all the years I have been buying pieces, I cannot think of anything I have run that has dropped out of an envelope, sent to me on spec. But I can think of many times when editors have sent on pieces with a suggestion that they are worth a look. At first glance these pieces are unexceptional. Some are barely literate. Only after a little research – a check on the writer's name, a look at the letter that came with it – does it become clear why the editor is taking such a close interest.

So, if you have an 'in', use it. Let us have no nonsense about not using connections or succeeding on your own merits. If you have an instantly recognizable name, or are well connected, or you can convey that you are fabulously good-looking, write to the editor. I particularly recommend doing this if you can drop in the proprietor's name and explain that he suggested you write.

The rest of you will have to remember that papers not only have members of staff but also a pool of existing freelances to call on. They have already paid for the staff writers and they know what their reliable freelances can do, so why would they pay to use you instead?

Because you have a close knowledge or a special insight, that's why. Or you are the first to spot the potential story.

You may not have a path straight to the editor, but you may know someone else on the paper or magazine. Pick their brains. Ask who runs which sections. Find out all you can about the people who commission work and how they operate. Unless the person you know is absolutely junior, ask if you can use his or her name when you first approach the paper, or, better still, get your friend to put in a word of introduction for you.

If you don't know anyone, you will have to do the same research from the outside. Get hold of the paper or magazine, identify the sections that run pieces you think you could do and ring up to find who runs them.

The switchboard will come up with some names, but it is worth checking further. Go through to the desk suggested and check that the names you have been given are indeed the ones you want. There, you may find a secretary or PA who can tell you how the boss likes to be pitched. On the phone? Letter? Email? If you do find you are talking to an assistant, make him or her your very best friend. Be polite and grateful. They have the power to put you through or explain that their bosses are in perpetual meetings. Don't, on the other hand, make yourself a pain. They also have the power to see that you do not get through.

What you shouldn't expect is a long talk about the pieces you would like to write. These are busy people. Establish that they are in the market for ideas and how they would like to receive them.

There is no point in lying about your experience – it's quite easy to find whether you really have written pieces for the *Express*'s features department – but nor should you present yourself as a complete beginner. If, on the other hand, you have done some 'work experience' somewhere, no one would think it too wicked if you change that into 'work'. Similarly, you are entitled to change a couple of pieces published somewhere into 'several' or 'quite a few' or to say that you write 'fairly regularly'.

But it is vital at this point to have that clear idea of the paper or magazine to which you are talking. Think of the pieces it runs. Can you see the piece you have in mind fitting into that category? Put yourself in the position of the commissioning editor: the piece about your feelings may fascinate you, but now that you are looking at it from their perspective, is it interesting?

This is the test where those striving to get into journalism so often let themselves down. Intelligent, entertaining, interesting people suddenly become tone-deaf, putting forward ideas that are quite unlike anything that appears in the paper they have approached.

You are a salesman or woman. You are cold-calling. There is a little window of opportunity. If you do not impress immediately, it will be slammed in your face. So you need a little of the cheek and a little of the charm and some of the technique of the man on the doorstep trying to flog the new vacuum cleaner.

Don't say: 'I'm working as an accountant but what I really want to be is a journalist and I thought you might be interested in some pieces I have written.' That sentence contains three messages guaranteed to turn off any self-respecting commissioning editor: 'accountant' (sombre-suited, boring and related to the gang currently investigating editorial expenses at the paper), 'I want to be a journalist' (I am not one) and 'pieces I have written' (a collection of student essays and several thousand words of adolescent opinion of the kind that fills web logs and clogs up the internet).

Do say: 'I write about young urban professionals and I think there is a terrific piece to be done on the drug tests which the big firms are introducing.' That sentence says you are a writer – without claiming that you get anything published – begins to sell me something – a 'terrific piece' – and promises revelation about a group that papers and magazines never fail to find interesting: young men and women working in big banks and spending their huge salaries on drugs. If you can work a little sex into it too, you are half-way there.

The best you can hope for at this stage is to provoke enough interest to be asked to flesh out your idea with a story outline. If it is not already on your computer, you should do it fast, so that the commissioning editor sees it before you are forgotten again. Fax it, email it: get it over now.

This outline is not the story. It explains what the story is and how you will write it. To take the example of drug tests at investment banks, will it name names? Do you have bankers who have agreed to be quoted? How widespread is the practice?

There is temptation at this point to flam up the story in order to get the commission. You should write the outline of the story you are confident you can produce, not of the story the paper would love to have. The latter course may guarantee you get invited to write the piece, but when it falls far short of what you have promised, you are unlikely to be asked to write again.

If you are working on rumour rather than fact, say so. If you have sources who will speak but who will not be named, say so. Your task is to sell the story hard enough for the newspaper to want the piece but not so hard that the end result disappoints. Only a foolish commissioning editor would use a story proposal as the basis for a big pitch at the paper's features conference, but if he does, and the story doesn't stand up, he will take it out on you.

The story outline goes down well. You are asked to write the piece. So that's a commission? Not necessarily. It all depends on the terms you discuss. Times are changing, not least because accountants are forcing journalists to run their papers in a more businesslike fashion, but there can still be much misunderstanding in the informal way in which work is commissioned.

You may be invited to write the piece 'to see how it works out'.

'You mean you want the piece?'

'Yes, I'd certainly like a look at it.'

'But you are paying me, yes?'

'Well, let's talk about that when it is written.'

On this basis, you are writing 'on spec'. The invitation to write the piece gives you the right to introduce yourself as a representative of the paper in your researches – and that makes things very much easier when you are talking to officialdom – but there is no guarantee that you will be paid for your work.

As in any business negotiation, only you can calculate how much power you have to get a better deal. If you are putting up a 'think piece' – that is to say, there is no research to do and you can knock it out relatively painlessly – it is probably worth producing it without any guarantee of money. But if this piece will take a week's research, you may decide you should not do it without negotiating at least some interim payment.

Bear in mind that you are just starting out and that getting a piece accepted is more important than the money. You are not doing this for charity, but you don't want to get bogged down now in an argument about what this story is worth. Treat these early pieces as 'loss leaders'. If this goes well, there will be others. Then will come the time to start getting serious about money.

Now *is* the time, however, to get clear what you are agreeing to do. Some publications – these tend to be magazines, which work to longer deadlines – confirm all details in a contract. Newspapers are more informal. Make sure that you have the name of the person who has commissioned you and that you know how many words are expected. You may not want to discuss money on these first pieces, but you should once you are writing more regularly. You should also be clear on whether you can claim necessary expenses for the work that you are doing. If this story involves some travel, for example, you must make sure that the paper knows that and expects to pay for it. Otherwise you are going to be out of pocket. Above all, be absolutely clear about the deadline.

As far as you are concerned, the deadline is not flexible. This piece may be for a Sunday newspaper that doesn't go to press until Friday, but if your deadline is Tuesday evening you get it in by Tuesday evening. Nothing marks you out as unprofessional faster than a failure to file on time.

Be clear too about how you are going to file the story. These days it is a waste of everyone's time to get 'hard copy' – the piece on printed sheets – posted in or faxed over. So you need to know which email address to use. Having sent it, you must not only ring in to check that the desk has the copy, but must also provide a number where the desk can reach you in case of queries.

Naturally, having just produced the piece, you expect the commissioning editor to be as interested in it as you are. For him or her, however, it is just one of many pieces due in. Don't expect to hear immediately. Do be available on the number you gave – or able to ring back – over the next few days. It is very frustrating in a newspaper office to have questions about a piece of copy and no one available to answer them.

In an ideal world, your piece is so good that it goes straight into the newspaper. It actually happens from time to time. This is the best result. The worst result is that you have produced a piece of unpublishable rubbish. The usual result is that there is enough in the piece to show that it will be good enough for the paper, but only after some extra work. This can be anything from a couple of extra quotes to a fundamental restructuring. As with your initial negotiation, it is important to discuss exactly what is required and how long you have got to do it.

At this point we should introduce some other words of warning. It is quite common for papers to take a piece by a freelance and pass them on to a staff writer to do further work. Sometimes – particularly when they are in the hands of news desks rather than feature departments – these pieces appear with no other name than the staffer's. It is irritating, but at least you still get your money. You may decide that the money is more important than the by-line, or to make it clear next time that this is a piece you want to write yourself, or to go to a paper that believes in giving by-lines to its freelance writers.

You may also encounter a nasty little device called the 'kill fee'. This is a payment newspapers offer when they decide not to run a piece. If the decision were based on the quality of the copy you could understand the principle. More often, the piece is presented to the paper just as promised and to the satisfaction of the commissioning editor. It just happens that there is no room in the paper, or the agenda has moved on, or another paper has tackled the same subject in between the commission and the production of the piece.

This is like no other commercial arrangement. Imagine ordering a suit from a tailor. You choose the cloth, he makes it to your specification and does the work to a high professional standard. But you decide that you do not like the colour you chose and tell him you will only pay him half the agreed fee. It wouldn't happen in tailoring. It still happens in journalism. Complain.

Finally, you must face the fear that the newspaper or magazine will look at your idea, turn it down and promptly give it to someone else to do. It does happen, though there is a greater sense of honour at most newspapers than you might imagine. There is also an element of self-interest on their part: if they steal your story, they know they will never get another one from you. Don't be paranoid about this. You may imagine that the idea you have just had for a story is unique. It is perfectly possible that someone at the newspaper has had it too. But be circumspect. If you are too guarded in your early conversations, it is impossible to put across the idea that you are trying to sell. But if you are trying to sell a news story, you should be cautious about revealing too much detail.

If, for instance, you have discovered that the controversial soap star whom the tabloids have been chasing for a week is living in your street, don't kick off your conversation with the news desk by telling them so: before you know where you are they will have traced your address through the reverse phone directory and a team of reporters will be on their way when you have barely put the phone down. You wouldn't be the first freelance to be told, in the middle of a negotiation about a story: 'Sorry, mate, we don't need you any more. We've got to the girl ourselves.'

If papers do not always seem to be entirely honest in their dealings, it is better to be straight yourself. If you are offering a news story, you should be clear that you are either keeping it exclusively for the paper to which you are talking, or offering it all around. News editors get very cross when they find that the story they thought they were getting to themselves has been sold to everyone.

News agencies work on the basis that most stories make more money from several small fees than one moderate one. They offer only their best stories exclusively, on the basis that they are good enough to attract a substantial payment.

Remember that all stories have a limited life. If you think you have an exclusive line to a big breaking story, you need to be on the phone now, not thinking about it for another week. And if you are on the phone, you also need to be ready to write it now. Scrap your other plans and make a name for yourself.

If you can only get that first piece under your belt, the world of journalism begins to look a less daunting place. Then you can begin to take stock and to work out the kind of stories that work for Sunday rather than daily papers, or the papers that look more generously on freelances.

People will often tell you that journalism is all about building up contacts. They mean the kind of contacts who might give you stories. But it is just as important to build up contacts with the people who might commission stories. As we discussed earlier in this chapter, all those newspaper executives need ideas: they are delighted to find someone who can supply them. Once things are going well, firm up the relationship by asking if you can come in for a chat. Make sure, when you meet, that you have read the paper carefully for the last week and bring a list of ideas with you. It shows you are trying. This is the time to start to discuss rates of pay. You may not be in a position to demand top dollar, but you can make sure that no one is taking advantage of you. This is also a great opportunity to put yourself in the forefront of the desk's imagination. We have been talking about stories that you put up: once you have established a relationship, you can become one of that happy group of writers to whom story lines are offered. They may not like your own idea on youth culture, for example, but there is another piece to do with youth that they would love you to do.

You will soon learn the rhythm of the paper or magazine – which are the quiet times of the day or week when commissioning editors are free to talk, which are the lean times of the year when they are desperate for ideas. If you can come up with a stream of ideas in the dog days of August, you can make yourself very popular.

Like all good sales agents, you will soon pick up the right tone. If you have terrific stories to sell, your manner doesn't matter. If your suggestions are less obviously brilliant, you need to find the balance between persistence and being a pain in the neck. Remember that it is always easier to visualize an idea that is reduced to a simple memo: use email to bombard the desk.

The best journalist I knew at this game operated before email, and used the fax. In fact he broke the rules I have outlined here and didn't bother to make initial contact, preferring to fire off faxes, addressed to me by name as news editor at the *Sunday Telegraph*. For a couple of weeks his faxes landed on my desk too late to use, having been round the then antiquated communications system of the office. This was a shame, for his ideas were brilliant. Typically, in any list of seven, one would be a stinker, two would be close to what we were already working on, three would be as good as anything on our own news list and one would be really clever.

I got to know Tom Quirk well. He was in his forties and had worked on Fleet Street and was now based in Birmingham, where he wrote the features he wanted to write and offered up the others as ideas, taking a tip-off fee for the ones we used. Tom collapsed and died while out running one evening. His imagination in developing story ideas put the rest of us to shame.

There may be times when you have ideas for stories that you cannot write yourself. You are too close to the subject, perhaps, and would be embarrassed to be seen writing about it. Or you have heard a fascinating piece of information but do not have the contacts to check it out. These are the pieces you should offer up as 'tips' or 'leads' or simply ideas. Papers depend on information like this. They will make sure you get paid for it.

Ah! The payment. Magazines tend to be efficient about paying, though they have an unpleasant habit of waiting until the piece appears in print before they do so. This can take weeks. Papers are moving to 'self-billing', which means they pay for work without receiving an invoice from you. But until they are all so efficient, you should get into the habit of invoicing for any work that you do, giving the name of the person who commissioned it and claiming the fee agreed.

Papers are often slow to pay. Sometimes this is policy: if they are not passing the money to you they can spend it on something else. More often it is just inefficiency. You have done the work; you should be paid. It is time to move on from the quiet, polite figure who rang up all those weeks ago. Complain. Ring the accounts department and try to track it down. Call the commissioning editor, the one who is now your friend, and make him or her feel guilty.

The last thing to think about is copyright. Unless you sign it away, you retain it, which means you get an extra payment if the work is syndicated or picked up and used by anyone else. Since the advent of the internet, this has become an increasingly contentious area, with papers and magazines commissioning on the basis that pieces will also be used on their websites. The National Union of Journalists advises its members that they should assert that their work is to appear only in paper form. Like all the negotiations we have discussed before, this is a matter for the relative power of the paper and the writer. Having been responsible for the *Daily Telegraph* website for some years, I developed a simple philosophy that those who did not choose to see their work on the website could choose to go elsewhere, an attitude embraced by most publishers. If you were the most sought-after writer in the world, or had the exclusive of the decade, you might be able to change my mind.

For examples of rates of pay, go to the website of the National Union of Journalists, www.nuj.org.uk. But remember that there are no rules. Journalism is show business and the market rules. The better you write, the cleverer your ideas, the faster you produce, the more you earn.

Loved and Loathed:
Insiders' Tips of Dos and Don'ts II

Sarah Sands, deputy editor and Saturday editor, the *Daily Telegraph*

Dos
- Cockiness (but see the traits that will make you loathed below)
- Offer to do anything – run errands, get tea, stand on doorsteps, night shifts, Sunday shifts
- Generosity – credit contributions from others (while making clear that the best work is yours)
- Drink with colleagues (but don't get a reputation as a drinker)
- Always look alert and ready
- Avoid becoming aggrieved when colleagues seem to be getting further than you
- Work harder
- Develop resilience – treat every setback as a springboard
- Humour – particularly black humour
- Use the gloominess of the old timers to emphasize your own cheerfulness

Don'ts
- Cockiness – you can have too much of it
- Moaning
- Negativity
- Looking for reasons why stories can't work rather than reasons why they can
- Getting yourself on the press junket to Barbados

Ruth Gledhill, religion correspondent, *The Times*

Dos
- Trust
- Accuracy
- Respect for others
- The ability to strive for impartiality, to put aside one's own prejudices for the duration of an inquiry
- Practise on the inside what you do on the outside. You don't have to like everyone but newspapers are diverse organizations, like cities, with their own centres, regions and suburbs. It is important to extend the same respect and consideration to colleagues that you do to contacts

Don'ts
- Unbridled ambition, such as the kind that prompts journalists to claim credit for a colleague's initiatives. Such people are sometimes referred to as 'by-line bandits'
- Blogging mercilessly about the activities of your colleagues
- Serious misquoting, by omission as well as commission, sufficient to alter radically the meaning
- Betraying the identity of a 'source'
- Becoming too grand, mistaking the coverage of celebrity for celebrity itself

Paul Rees, editor *Q* **magazine**

Dos
- The willingness to regularly work overtime without complaining
- The willingness to proof read and fact-check your own copy before submitting it to the subs' desk
- The willingness to say, 'I'll gladly do that', when it's clear

absolutely no one else is going to be mad/stupid enough to volunteer
- Nodding sagely and/or laughing manically at your immediate superior's musings, whatever they may be.
- Making the tea on a reliably consistent basis

Don'ts
- Doing the opposite to the above

5

Assembling the facts

One of the things that journalists and readers quarrel about is objectivity. Readers accuse journalists of writing a biased account: 'You've only given one side of the story.' 'You just wrote the story you wanted to write.' 'I don't know why I bothered speaking to you.' Sooner or later, someone in the newsroom quotes C. P. Scott, the man regarded as the author of the guiding principle on fact and opinion for newspapers: 'Comment is free, but facts are sacred.'

The words come from a celebrated essay on journalism published in 1921, by which time Scott had been editor of the *Guardian* – it was called the *Manchester Guardian* in those days – for forty-nine years. He went on to serve another eight. Journalists take his words to mean you can write what you like in the comment pages as long as you stick to facts in news. That's fine, except that you don't need a degree in media studies to know that the nature of 'fact' is highly contentious.

Even in the most innocent of areas, newspapers can move from the clearly factual to the highly contentious. I was usually confident that the elderly couples I was sent to see as a cub reporter had indeed been married for fifty years. That was a fact. But as soon as the sub-editor wrote the headline 'Tom and Dolly celebrate fifty golden years', his predictable pun may well have been putting a deceitful gloss on a wretched relationship. Did they regard those years as golden? In the mildest, most innocent way, 'golden' was comment.

There are stories in every paper that are clearly factual. If we are told that three people died in a car crash, we can believe that three people have indeed died. At the other end of the spectrum there are stories that are completely untrue. To give one of my favourite examples, there was no truth in the front-page story in the *Sun* revealing that the singer Elton John had paid a veterinary surgeon to remove the vocal chords of the guard dogs around his house, so that they would not keep him awake at night. Eventually, the *Sun* apologized, and paid out money in damages.

It is not that journalists necessarily set out to tell lies. In virtually every case, they believe what they write to be true, though by the time a story has gone through the editing process, with a news desk and sub-editors 'improving' it, a good story may have become a better story to the point where it is no longer entirely factual. There are occasions too when newspapers become so convinced by the accuracy of their source for a story that not even the most vehement denials can convince them they have got it wrong.

In between the completely right and the utterly wrong are hundreds of stories in which the degree of objective fact is higher or lower. Sometimes it goes down because of matters outside the control of the writer: the witnesses to whom the journalist speaks simply get it wrong. Sometimes the fault lies with the journalist: specific elements of the story are either given greater weight or there is no attempt to consider the other side of an issue. Sometimes the problem lies in the nature of news: there is not enough space to give the detail that would make a story more accurate.

Journalists are not always keen to acknowledge these difficulties, or not in public at any rate. But in our private moments we recognize a gnawing doubt that prevents our becoming too cocky about our ability to report objective fact: how often do we read a newspaper story on a subject of which we have close, personal knowledge and feel that it accurately conveys the situation in every detail? In my experience, hardly ever.

Some of these problems are to do with the writing – what you might call the cooking – and we will come to them later. For now, we are concerned with the information that goes into the story. This, you might say, is sourcing the ingredients. And as in cookery, the higher the quality of the ingredients, the better the eventual result.

There are general principles about gathering information that apply to all forms of journalism. It is vital to be accurate about detail. If you can't get the basics right, why should the reader believe anything else you write? British newspapers have developed specific demands. They expect to print full names, ideally with ages and occupations. It's no good filing a story about a Mr K. Fletcher; make sure you get his full name. But if you have failed to find out an age or an occupation, say so. There's no point in weakening your piece by taking a guess. You may get an easier ride from the commissioning editor, but only until he or she finds out you made it up.

Take nothing for granted: some Smiths spell their name Smyth, Philips often takes a second 'l', Anns go with and without 'e's and Janes sometimes slip in a 'y'. There are little traps like these in almost every name. It may not mean much to you, but it does to the person whose name you misspell. In a simple story, getting names wrong merely irritates. In complex and contentious stories, minor mistakes undermine the whole work. Even if the main thrust of the story is right, little errors suggest that it might not be.

Imagine if a story of yours ever came to court in a libel action. Think of the fun a barrister would have in taking a jury through a story that is full of minor mistakes. How, he would ask, can we trust this writer on any of the detail in the story?

From the moment you start speaking to people, whether it's face to face, on the phone – or, too often nowadays, by email – get into the habit of checking these details. Check too that what you think you already know is right. There is no guarantee that anything you read is accurate. Once they have made it into print, mistakes tend to be there for good, read and repeated by every journalist who comes after. So, short of checking with the Prince of Wales that he is indeed son of the Queen and next in line for the throne, take nothing for granted.

You must also get used to keeping proper notes of all your conversations and interviews. If you are writing a basic, straightforward story you will find it useful to have the material in one place. If you are writing a story that might be challenged, you will find it is vital. Always remember the possibility of that court case, with lawyers arguing over every verb in every sentence. If you haven't got notes or tapes of your interviews, made at the time and legible to others, you will be in trouble.

In 2003 the British government called on the judge Lord Hutton to inquire into the circumstances of the death of a government scientist, David Kelly, who killed himself after discovering that he was to be revealed as the source of BBC stories about British intelligence on Iraqi weapons of mass destruction, shortly before the United States and Britain went to war in Iraq. Lord Hutton's inquiry called all the journalists involved for questioning in public. Suddenly every phone call, meeting and note – or lack of note – was under the scrutiny of the whole world.

Some of us looked on rather fearfully, conscious that our own care of notes often left much to be desired. We remembered follow-up phone calls written up on scraps of newspaper, or big doodles across pages of notebooks containing important quotes. It's easy to get it right when you are in command of the timetable and making all your calls with your notebook or tape recorder ready. It gets harder when the man you are looking for rings you back when you are heading out of the house for work or it is the middle of the day and you've a sandwich spread across your desk.

Nevertheless, the more trouble you take to get into good habits from the start, the more keeping notes becomes second nature. It doesn't actually matter if they are on a scrap of newspaper – as long as you put the scrap with the main file.

The Hutton Inquiry was an exceptional case. The stories written and broadcast about the government had been highly contentious. But the principle applies to the most mundane stories. You may be tempted, once a piece is published, to throw away the notes and move on to the next. Don't. It could take weeks for someone, somewhere, to take issue with what you have written. You may well need those notes again. Editors will defend everything you have written – provided you have got the evidence to back up what you wrote.

Unless you have fantastic shorthand – so good that you know you can read it back as easily as handwriting – transcribe your notes as soon as you can. I thought I was a shorthand whiz, but unless I quickly transcribed the relevant bits alongside my Teeline note, I swiftly lost the thread. If you tape your interviews, keep the tapes.

Nothing deflates an angry reader faster than the proof that he did indeed use the words that he now contests. Nothing, on the other hand, encourages him more than the knowledge you have no notes. If you ever get involved in a libel case, you will be astonished at the depth of the inquiry into notes, phone calls and interviews. We shall talk more about the law in another chapter. For the moment, let's just repeat the point: you will take notes of interviews and you will keep those notes.

But perhaps we are getting ahead of ourselves. Whom are you speaking to, and why? Put most simply, you should be speaking to anyone who can provide information for your stories. That can mean, at one end, a police press officer whose job it is to provide information to reporters or, at the other, a senior official in a government organization who is not meant to talk to the press.

The status of that individual has implications for how openly he or she can speak, whether he or she agrees to be quoted by name and whether what he or she says can be treated as fact. If we stay, for the moment, with the idea of a basic story – a road accident, say, that has killed a family – then your first conversations should be straightforward transactions. You ring the police press office and explain that you are writing a story about the crash. The police press office tells you what happened.

There, you now have enough information to write a story. But could you do better?

Well, if you were working for a local paper, you would certainly be expected to try. Perhaps if you chatted up the police press officer a little, he might reveal some detail about the dead family, and if you were also to ring the Fire Brigade, you might get a little more information. Firefighters tend to attend the same accident scenes as the police, but because they are not involved in the law in the same way, they are often much more talkative.

You might also discover, in the course of these inquiries, that the accident happened at a well-known blackspot. There are, perhaps, local residents who witnessed the crash or came out to help or who have been campaigning for better road markings or for a speed limit. Then there are the relatives of the dead family. With extra work, you might be able to transform a road crash story into a bigger, human-interest article.

This is how stories build. What starts as an everyday story can become something bigger or more interesting if only you ask the right questions. You might be patting yourself on the back to see your straightforward account of the accident in print. But you would be less happy if, at the end of the week, the local weekly paper came out with a heartbreaking account of the family tragedy, revealing that they had been due to emigrate next day to Australia.

Here, as with all stories, you have to decide how much time you have to do such extra work. It is no good, when a daily paper expects the copy by 4 o'clock, to embark on the kind of inquiry that will take days. You need to weigh up what your commissioning editor expects, how long you have to do the story and, if you are going to make any money as a freelance, what kind of return you might get for the additional effort. Sometimes it makes sense to settle for the basic story on the first day and decide to pursue further information as a follow-up. Frequently the follow-up never happens: you will find there are many stories that start promisingly but lead nowhere.

How do you convince people to tell you things? All you can do is find the method that suits you. I have worked with reporters who are so charming that the villains they talk to are practically grateful for being exposed. I have worked with reporters who cannot carry on an interview with the most benign press officer without it ending in a shouting match. Both methods seem to work. You will soon find the one that suits you.

There is, however, a rather worrying trend for journalists to believe that they have to practise belligerence. This is what we might call the Jeremy Paxman school of journalism, after that TV presenter's highly confrontational style on BBC2's *Newsnight*. It is characterized by the question: why is this lying bastard lying to me? The technique works well for Mr Paxman, particularly when he is dealing with politicians, who are now usually pretty unpopular with viewers. But too many young journalists working in less combative fields now feel that the best way either to get the story or to get noticed is to be rude. It isn't.

There is also much journalistic folklore about getting stories while posing as other people. A friend of mine succeeded brilliantly in getting into a hospital and as far as the private-wing door of a young woman at the centre of a story simply by borrowing a white coat and posing as a doctor. Another colleague managed to get information about the bank account of Denis Thatcher, husband of the then Prime Minister, by posing as a member of staff at another branch. But those escapades are frowned on these days and largely forbidden under the code of conduct of the Press Complaints Commission. Unless you can establish an overriding public interest in your trying subterfuge – there is no other means of establishing important information – you should present yourself as a journalist from the start.

Remember that there are some items of information to which you are entitled and others that you will get only if the source chooses to tell you. This is where you need to develop some of the skills of the door-to-door salesman or the woman from the call centre. The longer you can keep them talking, the more they are likely to tell you something interesting.

Face to face? Or on the phone? Once again, there is a balance to be struck. How long do you have to do the piece? Is there something you are likely to get only by appearing in person? Time may not be on your side and it may seem a long way to go without the guarantee that the person will speak to you, but you will find you almost invariably get more from knocking on a door and speaking face to face than from asking the same questions on the phone.

The face-to-face talk may come after ringing up to arrange it. Or it may mean turning up without warning. There are many people who refuse to talk if approached on the phone but open up if you track them down to their homes.

How you get in, once they have answered the door, is up to you. I remember, when I worked in Sheffield, a successful tabloid reporter who covered the North of England for one of the nationals, who liked to play on the sympathy of the householders on whom he called. He would throw himself to his knees and sob that he would be thrown out of work if he did not return with the interview. It wasn't the proudest way to go about business, but it got results. They seemed particularly upset to see him rolling in the dirt in a smart white suit, which was unusual wear in the North at that time.

There is something in face-to-face contact that encourages people to talk. This, after all, is why door-to-door salesmen can make a living. A witness may recall more as you sit there over a cup of tea. He or she may come up with the names of other people to whom you can speak. By developing this relationship, you can make him or her more than a witness. Being supportive can make you the first person he or she thinks of calling if there is some development in the story.

Sadly, the speed of modern communications is encouraging many journalists to resort to email as a substitute for phone or face-to-face conversation. It should be a last resort rather than the first option. Emails are easy to ignore – most people find it harder to put down the phone on you or slam the door in your face than you would imagine – and, if they are answered at all, allow the interviewee more time to consider his or her answers than is helpful.

Are you better taking notes? Or taping your interviews? Yet again, this depends on the circumstances. If you are writing a news story, you may not need the detailed quotes that a tape recorder gives you. What's more, remember that it is going to take at least as long as the original interview to play back the tape. If you are working against the clock, you are probably better off with written notes.

On the other hand, you may not be entirely confident in your note-taking, and a barely legible mixture of shorthand and scrawled words is not a great record. Some journalists find that taking a note prevents the natural flow of a conversation, and prefer to put a tape on the table. For feature pieces, or interviews, where you are anxious to convey your interviewee's manner of speaking, it is certainly easier to use a tape. There are, it should be said, no rules in newspapers that prevent your taping conversations without saying so. Here, newspaper reporters are better off than those who work in television and radio: broadcasters are able to use clandestine tapes only in certain circumstances. You, if you wish, can tape every phone call you make, without warning those to whom you talk. Before you do so, you might pause to consider their reaction if they find out.

Whenever you set out on a story, you have to believe that it is there to be brought in. But you also need to retain a degree of scepticism that acknowledges that you might be setting off on a wild goose chase. Every day, any number of tantalizing stories swim into the consciousnesses of news desks, commissioning editors and journalists. Many, alas, never amount to anything more than gossip. And while we all know that gossip is not always true, you can have a very hard time trying to persuade a news desk of that.

To give you an example, when I came to London to find news shifts on national papers in 1981, the first place I found work was the *Daily Mail*. The paper had a reputation for driving its reporters hard – it still does – but was always renowned too for trying out new talent. You didn't get paid much, but you did gain experience fast.

After a few weeks of night shifts, I was given a try-out on days and was sent off to Wimbledon to bring in the big one: with only a few days until the start of the Open Tennis Championship, the ball boys were about to go on strike in protest at the way they were being treated by some of the professional players.

This, if you think about it, is not the easiest story to stand up. The ball boys – there are ball girls as well nowadays – were drawn from London schools. It was unlikely that the schools would help. Any attempt to get hold of the names and addresses of the boys would have been treated with justifiable suspicion. As for the All England Lawn Tennis Club itself, it was notorious for its snobbish, unhelpful approach to all except accredited tennis correspondents. And the accredited tennis correspondents, of course, always behaved as though they owed more of a duty to Wimbledon than to reporters from the newsroom.

The only thing to do was hang around outside in the hope of getting some of the boys to talk. But, there were security guards at all the gates. There were policemen wandering around the perimeter. Perhaps there was not quite the paranoia around about paedophilia in 1981 that there is today, but I did not feel at ease as I loitered around the hedges outside the club. I guessed it would be marginally better to be arrested as an intruder than as a child molester.

To my surprise, I managed to stop a few of the boys as they came out and ask them how they were getting on. They were very excited about the forthcoming tournament. Were they enjoying themselves? Oh yes. Had anyone been horrid to them? Oh no. Was it true that they were threatening to go on strike? Certainly not. They could not imagine a greater honour than to be at Wimbledon.

I rang the news desk and told the assistant news editor that his story did not stand up.

'At the moment, they just seem very excited about the whole thing. Perhaps after a couple of days of the tournament, when they are tired and they have been shouted at and had balls blasted at them, they will feel a little differently.'

'How many ball boys have you spoken to?'

'About six.'

'And how many ball boys are there?'

'I'm not sure. About thirty, I think.'

'And you are telling me that this story does not stand up after speaking to just six? Get back in there and ask the other twenty-four.'

Fortunately I was leaving at the end of the week for a job on the *Sunday Times*. I told the assistant news editor I had had enough. This is a trivial example, but typical of the difficulty you can have in establishing that what sounds like a brilliant story is actually true.

The trouble is not so much that people make things up, but that pieces of gossip that start off with a kernel of truth can become embellished to the point of fantasy. Like urban myths – the mouse bones in the take-away meal, the child stolen by gypsies in the department store, the dead grandfather strapped to the roof rack of the car – they are often tantalizingly close, but prove elusive when you try to track them down.

Part of the problem is that people feel free to talk about things to friends, but balk at the thought of repeating the detail to a reporter. Or stories get passed on from private conversations and dinner parties, where it would threaten a friendship or breach social convention to give the name of the person spreading the story to a reporter.

This leads to the frustration of being unable to go to the source of the story. He or she may well be horrified that it is to be made public and deny all knowledge of something they were discussing openly only a day before.

In situations such as these, you have to build up roundabout routes of getting to the information that you want. To go directly to the people concerned is likely to invite a denial. You probably don't want to speak to them until you are sure that you have the story anyway.

Let's think of an example. You hear that the daughter of a Government minister has been suspended from university for dealing in drugs. The politician has often spoken on law and order. If his daughter is involved in illegal drugs, it is certainly interesting, and probably a story that is in the public interest. Indeed, as she is over eighteen, the mere fact of her being involved in an activity that is illegal makes her fair game.

Now, you could go straight to the politician and ask him. He may even tell you. But he may say: 'I make it a policy never to discuss anything to do with members of my family.' You can try to track down the daughter, but that could take days. And if you do find her, what if she says she doesn't know what you are talking about? If you speak to the university, the university will say it never discusses individual students. You try the local police, and they tell you they have no information on any drugs arrest. You track down the person who has been putting the story about, but that source clams up as soon as he or she knows that the press is looking at it.

To make things even more complicated, you know that speaking to any of those connected with the student will alert her family to the fact that the press is on to it. This may lead the family to make a public statement that prevents your getting the story as an exclusive. But you also know that if you have heard the story, other journalists may have heard it too. So you cannot be too leisurely in your inquiries for fear that someone else will get to the story first. Finally, you must remember that you do not have the powers of the police to go and ask questions. People may speak to you, but they certainly don't have to.

This is not the kind of story that you can run without confirmation. Imagine the trouble if you write up the rumour that the girl is suspended for a drugs offence and it turns out that she is away from university because she is sick, or because her mother is ill.

Instead you have to try to stand it up by alternative means – talking to fellow students perhaps, possibly by roping in student journalists at the same university – until you are sufficiently confident in your facts to approach the university or the family not as a supplicant, asking if something is true, but in the matter-of-fact way of those who know they already have the information they need.

You will be surprised how much more readily people respond to a statement of fact than to a question. You want to give them as little chance as possible to avoid the issue.

Look at the possibilities: 'I've heard a rumour that your daughter is home at the moment from university. Can you tell me if it is true that she has been suspended for a drugs offence?'

'Your daughter has been suspended from university for a drugs offence. Does her suspension in any way alter your views as a government minister?'

The problem with the first question is that you do not sound at all confident of your ground. The minister could easily say: 'I've long made it a rule never to discuss rumours and never to discuss my family. Goodbye.' He hasn't knocked the story down, but he has hardly stood it up. In asking the second question, you imply such certain knowledge that he must feel the story is going to come out. Unless, of course, it is wrong, in which case he is all the more likely to say so.

A brinkmanship has now developed between journalists and the people about whom they wish to write in news stories. There are many stories that it would be legally impossible to run without putting them to the subject of the story. But if you put the story to the subject too early, he or she may take steps either to prevent it coming out or to put a different gloss on it to other papers, destroying the impact of your own.

Imagine, for instance, that you have a story that affects the head of a big, well-known, public company. You have a sworn affidavit from a high-class escort girl who says that the company chief, a married man, has been hiring her for sex and paying with his corporate credit card. She gives a full account of their evenings together and produces credit-card slips that are indeed in the name of his company credit card. On the face of it, this is a pretty shocking use of shareholders' money.

There are, of course, other possible explanations. The man she has been seeing may claim to have been the company boss; he may even be an employee of the same company who has got hold of the chief's credit card. It could even be a plot by rivals to discredit him.

Therefore, at some point before running the story, you have to put the allegations to him. Leave it too late and you miss him. Do it too soon and – assuming the story is true – he has time to call in his media advisers and set in train a series of responses that range from seeking an injunction to prevent you running your story on the basis that it is a breach of his privacy, to writing a cheque to his company for the escort fees and going to a rival newspaper to get a sympathetic hearing for his 'sex shame' confession.

These are all fine judgement calls. What suits the handling of one story may not suit another. But if you are working in this kind of area, you should be aware of the pitfalls, think of what you have got and call on the help of experienced colleagues or newspaper lawyers in standing up your story.

There are times when the kind of story we have been discussing is a much more complicated affair than the accusation of wrongdoing by an individual. Sometimes you need to mount a complex investigation that may take weeks to come to fruition. There is a special term for this kind of inquiry: investigative reporting. It tends to go in and out of fashion, promoted by the excitement of great stories such as Watergate, which ended with the downfall of an American president, and relegated by the paper's accountants, who do not like the idea of a team of journalists working on stories that may never be written.

That, in a nutshell, is the problem with investigations. There may not, at the end, be a story. An investigation may involve anything from a single journalist to an entire team. It may centre on a story that is clearly there to be written – for instance, what was the secret intelligence that encouraged Tony Blair to go to war in Iraq in 2003? – or a kind of journalistic fishing expedition that is prompted by a tip-off – perhaps that a certain police officer has been taking bribes.

The inquiries that follow could take weeks or even longer. Unlike the police, journalists have no means of making people talk to them. There is little in journalism that is more rewarding if laborious inquiries lead to a fine story. Equally, few things are more draining of morale when they don't.

You should also ask yourself how interesting the story will be to readers if it stands up: I have met many reporters who become so immersed in their inquiries that they forget that the end result has to be a story that people will read. Sometimes the story becomes so arcane and the level of alleged wrongdoing so difficult to explain that the story is of little general interest despite all the work that has gone into it.

There are a number of special techniques that you will learn as you go along. Some of them may involve things as dramatic as surveillance and subterfuge. Others demand an extensive knowledge of the kind of information that is publicly available through filings such as company returns, the electoral register and registrations of births, marriages and deaths.

You will find that fellow journalists are usually eager to help: if you have what seems like a good story but you are not sure how to go about standing it up, get the news desk to put an experienced journalist on the case with you. You may have to share the by-line at the end, but it could make the difference between the story getting into print or limping along unresolved.

Those special techniques apart, you should make sure that your inquiry is meticulously organized. Draw up plans of exactly what you need to establish and how you might go about it. Keep careful notes of every conversation. Discuss with colleagues how to proceed. Go through the possible scenarios that follow any line of questioning and ask yourself constantly: could there be an innocent explanation for this? Is there another way this could have happened? Is what is happening illegal, morally reprehensible or just quite interesting if you happen to have certain political or social beliefs?

Remember too that some of those who respond most helpfully to your questions may do so for reasons other than getting out the truth. You may not be able to tell immediately that they are lying, but by cross-checking information with your notes, you can find them out. Just as reporters adopt different techniques for dealing with interviewees, so people such as PR men can vary from the oleaginous to the brusque to the downright threatening. You should treat it as a badge of honour the first time someone tells you: 'You should know that I am a very good friend of your proprietor.' Sometimes it is even true. Don't be afraid, but do take the precaution of discussing the claim with your editor.

We discussed earlier the danger of believing everything you read in the cuts – the name we still give to previously published stories – whether they are in actual cuttings form or in an electronic library or on the internet. Those previous stories may not have got things right, but you should always have a look through them before embarking on any story of your own.

They may reveal that the story you are working on has already been written. They will almost certainly give you background information about the people or the subject you intend to write about. Experts find it extremely irritating to have a reporter come to see them who knows nothing about their subject. They are more likely to treat seriously someone who knows at least the basics of the background. Not only can they be a little more confident that you will get things right, but they are saved the trouble of going into the background at great length.

Take care, however, when you go through the cuts that you pick up background information rather than the words themselves. Those fine phrases are someone else's, and if you start copying them out it's plagiarism. You don't want to get a reputation for stealing another journalist's words, and you can bet your life that someone, somewhere, will notice.

There is nothing wrong, on the other hand, with using others' words when you admit that they are not your own. The *Daily Telegraph* theatre critic, Charles Spencer, said of a performance by the actress Nicole Kidman that it was 'theatrical Viagra', a phrase that appeared in every interview with Ms Kidman for the following year. But because the description was attributed to Charles Spencer, that was fine.

Talking of show business, that is the other area where research is vital. You can, just, get away with not knowing too much about a news story until you get involved in it. But go to interview an actor about a film, an author about his book or a company director about his business without having done your homework, and you are sunk.

You should prepare for these occasions as a barrister prepares for a difficult court case. See their work, read their books, learn about their companies. Check out what has been written about them before. Ask colleagues who know them what they are like. Then work out in advance what you want to ask them. These are the set-piece occasions where you are likely to want to use a tape recorder rather than inhibit the flow by taking notes. But carry a note of the questions you want to ask and, vitally, listen to the answers.

Some interviewers are so determined to plough through their prepared questions that they fail entirely to listen to the answers. The boss of a big company could practically confess to murdering his wife and still have his interviewer return to the office with answers on the corporate profits. If they are telling you something more interesting than the questions you are asking, perhaps it is worth letting them get on with it.

So finally, you have notebooks of information, tapes of interviews, pages of facts you have discovered. It is time to turn them into a story.

6

Practical writing

Here are the ways in which five different newspapers began their main front-page stories the day after Prince William and Prince Harry issued a statement condemning the former royal butler Paul Burrell for writing a book about their mother. The statement came at the end of a week in which the *Daily Mirror*'s revelations had made big news and the paper had sold as many as 200,000 extra copies a day by publishing extracts from the book.

The *Sun*: 'Furious Prince William last night ordered Paul Burrell: Shut up – and stop betraying my mother.'

The *Daily Mail*: 'Prince William last night accused Paul Burrell of a "cold and overt betrayal" of Princess Diana.'

The *Guardian*: 'The royal princes, William and Harry, launched a devastating assault on Princess Diana's former butler, Paul Burrell, last night following a week of tabloid revelations from private letters disclosed in a book to be published next week.'

The *Daily Telegraph*: 'Prince William and Prince Harry accused Paul Burrell, their mother's former butler, of a "cold and overt betrayal" last night and pleaded with him to halt his distressing revelations about Diana, Princess of Wales.'

The *Daily Mirror*: 'Paul Burrell has agreed to meet Princes William and Harry after they attacked his book on Princess Diana.'

The main front-page story is called the 'lead' or the 'splash'. The first paragraph is called the 'intro'. These intros may not have appeared exactly as they were written: a sub-editor is likely to have rewritten the reporter's paragraph in the case of the tabloid papers, the *Sun* and the *Mail*. The broadsheet versions are probably closer to the reporters' original copy.

You can see instantly the difference in style between the three tabloid and the two broadsheet papers. This is not just a matter of the length of the paragraph but also of the direct language in which it is couched. We will go into that language shortly, and see that the tabloid *Mail* has actually written a more objective intro than the broadsheet *Guardian* and *Telegraph*.

First, let us look at the underlying structure of the paragraphs, from which we can see that all the papers conform here to the basic principles of a hard-news intro.

These principles are that a hard-news story starts with most, and often all, of the 'five Ws' – who, what, why, where and when. Let us dissect the stories above. Someone has done something, for a reason, at a time and in a place.

Who? Prince William/Prince William and Prince Harry/The royal Princes. Or, in the *Mirror*'s story, Paul Burrell.

What? Ordered Paul Burrell/accused Paul Burrell/launched an assault on Paul Burrell. Or, again the different line in the *Mirror*, agreed to meet the Princes.

Why? Because of his 'cold and overt betrayal'.

Where? You'll have to go down the page to discover that – the stories explain that the Princes attacked the butler in a statement.

When? Last night. Or, in the *Mirror* story, after they attacked the butler's book.

You will have noticed that the *Mirror* took a different line on the story from its rivals. It reversed the order of the story – making Paul Burrell the subject and the Princes the object – because it had been running exclusive stories from Mr Burrell's book all week. He was the man in the news and he was 'owned' by the *Mirror*, making him the *Mirror*'s own character. No one else could talk to him at this time and in getting his reaction to the attack by the Princes, the paper was able to put a different slant on a story that everyone had.

The fact that the story had been running all week also explains why the 'why' is missing from the *Sun*'s intro. The details from Mr Burrell's book about the Princess had already attracted huge attention. There was no need to spell out what was going on in the background, to explain why Prince William was speaking in this way to Paul Burrell, because readers already knew that there was controversy involving the Royal Family and Mr Burrell.

The 'why clause' appears soon enough, however – in the second paragraph of the *Sun*'s story: 'William, 21, tore into Burrell *as the greedy ex-butler prepared to publish a tell-all book about Princess Diana on Monday.*'

That prior knowledge on the part of readers is reflected in the wording of headlines and straplines. Anyone picking up a paper after a week on Mars would have been puzzled: Wills and Harry tell Paul Burrell: SHUT UP (the *Sun*); Prince accuses Burrell of 'cold and overt betrayal': THE WRATH OF WILLIAM (*Daily Mail*); Princes vent fury at butler (the *Guardian*): 'A cold and overt betrayal'; William and Harry condemn ex-butler's 'deeply painful' revelations about their mother (the *Daily Telegraph*); I'LL MEET THE BOYS (*Daily Mirror*).

You may also notice an old habit of newspapers, which is to use 'last night' as much as possible, in the belief that it makes the story more immediate. Total accuracy would have demanded the words 'yesterday afternoon', which is when the statement from the Princes was actually made public, but that would not have sounded quite as dramatic.

I've seen reporters sit racking their brains for the right intro. You can waste a huge amount of effort trying to start a news story other than through the who-what-why-where-when approach. If it doesn't work, it could be because you are not writing a news story at all.

Here is the form at its purest, in an intro from the *Manchester Evening News*: 'A motorist died after his BMW was involved in a collision with a Honda Civic in Hale, near Altrincham on Saturday night.'

Who? A motorist (to use his name here would slow down the story, but it appears later on). What? Died. Why? Because his car hit another one. Where? Hale. When? Saturday night. So much information conveyed in just twenty-one words, even down to the makes of the two cars in the crash.

While we are analysing the words, we might notice the use of 'in a collision with'. Generations of news reporters have been taught to use this construction because it does not impute blame. If we write 'collided with' we are said to imply that whoever did the colliding caused the crash. I am sceptical about the difference, but if it keeps news editors and newspaper lawyers happy . . .

The WWWWW principle works in papers around the world. Look at these examples, taken at random on a November day, from – in order – the *Baltimore Sun*, the *Times of India* and the *Australian*. As we saw earlier, the 'why' does not always appear.

'An evening of Hallowe'en merriment ended in bloodshed Friday when an Anne Arundel County police officer shot and killed his estranged wife's boyfriend at the family's Millersville home and then fatally shot himself.'

'Ghaziabad police arrested seven sex workers, and a woman kingpin, along with six clients, from the city's elite Ramprastha area on Delhi–Uttar Pradesh border on Friday night.'

'A US Chinook helicopter carrying dozens of troops was shot down as it flew towards Baghdad airport last night, killing at least 13 soldiers and injuring more than 20 others in the deadliest day for American forces in the six-month-old occupation of Iraq.'

You may feel that working all these elements into your intro makes it unwieldy. There was certainly a lot going on in Millersville the night of 31 October. Sometimes you may feel you should break down the elements into the first two or three paragraphs. But on the principle that you wish to communicate clearly and logically with your readers, so that they know from the beginning what this story is about, it is worth trying to work everything in at the start.

Now let us go back and look at the language used in our British examples earlier. The *Sun* has taken the statement from Prince William and turned it into a more vivid form of direct speech. He did not say 'shut up', though it was the gist of his message. Using the language in this way sets up the idea of a direct, almost physical confrontation between the Prince and the butler.

The intro to the *Mail* story is remarkably objective. The paper uses no adjectives – the Prince was furious in the *Sun* – and uses the direct quote, 'cold and overt betrayal'. Interestingly, the two broadsheets quoted here, both of which would claim to provide a more objective news coverage than that of the *Mail*, throw in a number of phrases and adjectives designed to dramatize the story.

The Princes haven't just issued a statement, they have 'launched an assault'. What's more, the *Guardian* announces that this assault is 'devastating', though how it knows what effect it has had on Mr Burrell is puzzling. It certainly hasn't had a chance to speak to him, because he has been tied up all week with the *Daily Mirror*, which is paying to serialize his book. He did make a statement in response to that from the Princes, when I have to say he did not sound devastated.

In the *Daily Telegraph*, the Princes' request to Mr Burrell – 'We ask Paul please to bring these revelations to an end' – has become 'pleaded', a word that carries more emotional overtones, and the revelations 'distressing'. There is good reason to write 'distressing', for the Princes say in their statement that Mr Burrell's actions are 'deeply painful'. But the use of 'pleaded' makes a judgement about the relative power of the protagonists and emphasizes for emotional effect the relative youth of the Princes.

Journalists tend to snort at this kind of analysis of words. The point is to get the story across, they argue, and all these intros do just that. But the more precise you can be about language, the more careful about separating what appears to be fact from what is actually comment, the more accurately your story will read.

Some words now exist almost entirely in newspapers. When, for instance, did you ever talk with your friends about 'sex romps'? They are things that exist only outside marriages, and only in the language of journalists. No one knows or cares what husbands and wives do with each other, but if either spouse sleeps with someone else, it is a 'sex romp'.

Don't worry, it is almost inevitable that you pick up a number of words and phrases that the industry uses all the time and use them like building blocks in your stories. Within weeks of starting at the *Star* in Sheffield, I had fire engines 'racing to the scene' and victims 'rushed to hospital'. Councillors were soon 'giving the green light to' new buildings, every assault was 'vicious' and, after a local security scare, police were naturally on 'red alert'. Even as I wrote it, I felt it unlikely that red warning lights were going on in police stations all over South Yorkshire, but I had the deputy news editor at my elbow and he seemed to like it. When you are working against the clock on an evening paper, perhaps filing over the phone to copy takers who are typing up the story even as you compose it, you waste too much time by pausing to come up with alternatives. But once you start looking carefully through your cuttings, you will be horrified to see how reliant you can be on cliché.

If it is a trait that is just about forgivable when you are writing against the clock, there is no excuse at other times. Cliché suggests you aren't bright enough or can't be bothered to think of something more original. When did you last read a piece about the rapper Eminem without the words 'controversial rapper' appearing? In 2004, when the Barclay brothers were bidding for the *Daily Telegraph*, I wondered whether any journalist covering the story would avoid the description 'the reclusive Barclay brothers'. I don't believe any did. Fortunately, good news editors recognize cliché. You might be lucky enough to get one who points it out in your first pieces. Mine did, crossing out the words 'small fortune' that I had used to describe the money a man had left to the local dogs' home rather than to his family. 'How much is a small fortune?' he asked. He was right. The trouble is, in constantly trying to ramp up the level of excitement in our use of language, we often merely succeed in reducing all stories to a similar level.

While I think of that news editor, I should pass on the other most important lesson he taught me, when he discovered that I had arrived in the office one hot summer day wearing a tie, but without a jacket. 'The Lord Mayor of Sheffield could die of a heart attack this morning,' he explained. 'And you would have to go down to write the story. Do you believe you could turn up without a jacket?' There may be stories you work on where it makes sense to dress down, but if in doubt, wear the kind of inoffensive suit, shirt and tie that will not put you at any disadvantage anywhere. Last time I checked with friends at the *Daily Mail*, women reporters were still banned from wearing trousers.

But we digress. Let us go back to that *Manchester Evening News* story: A motorist died after his BMW was involved in a collision with a Honda Civic in Hale, near Altrincham on Saturday night.

You don't actually need any more. It has a certain factual perfection. But papers have a way of dressing things up, however superfluously. In other hands, that 'collision' would have become a 'horror collision', as if you need the adjective once you have established that a man has died. In a smaller city, where fatal road accidents are less common than in Manchester, the story would have been spiced up not so much with extra drama as with dramatic-sounding words: 'A Saturday night out turned to tragedy for a Manchester man when . . .' Was it really necessary?

It is a good principle that if your story is good enough, it will tell itself. Fatal crashes are bad enough without being turned into 'horror smashes' or 'heartbreaking tragedies'. Go through your work and check how many words you have put in that don't need to be there. Then take them out.

But we are getting ahead of ourselves. Even before you start to write, work out what it is that you are trying to say. Imagine, for a moment, that you are telling your friends something that has happened. You start off with the crux, explain the implications and then go on to say how it happened. It's just the same with a news story.

Your most important points must come at the start, with secondary information coming later and more minor elements of detail coming at the end. News stories are not short stories with a dramatic twist at the end. They are written to be cut, if necessary, from the bottom, so if you leave important points too late in the story you will either irritate the sub-editor, who suspects you have missed the whole point and moves the later stuff further up, or see it disappear, for reasons of space.

Keep your points as simple as you can. Let them build, bit by bit, into the whole picture. The reader has a page of stories competing for attention. You may not always be able to make yours the most obviously interesting, but you can keep him or her going by writing in a way that is easy to follow. And remember: keep the language neutral. If the news is good enough, it speaks for itself. If it isn't, no amount of flam can make it so.

As you go through this story, introduce your characters, locations and organizations clearly. Make sure the people have first and second names, that places are identified and organizations spelt out in full, rather than given initials that your reader might not understand.

Avoid jargon. Many of the people to whom you talk may use it, but it doesn't mean that you have to. The police may talk about apprehending the suspected perpetrator; you can write about catching the suspect. Councils refer to housing stock; you can write about council houses. The solution, again and again, is to think of the language that newspaper readers would use.

You may yourself be expert in a subject, but you must remember that the readers are not. If your piece assumes a level of similar, specialized knowledge, you will lose them. Always remember that you are writing for the general reader. The *Daily Mirror* once worked on the principle that every story should be capable of being enjoyed and understood by the wife of a Sheffield bus driver. The reference may not work so well in the twenty-first century – and different papers have different audiences – but the point was well made.

Your story will benefit from direct quotes, which move it along. But there is no point in quotes that merely confirm what you have already written. You would be surprised how often I have seen copy like this: 'The police spokesman said officers were not looking for anyone else in connection with the death. "We are not looking for anyone else in connection with the death," he said.' Good news subs pounce on repetition such as this. Don't give them reason to.

And tie up loose ends. There is more than one side to any story. Make sure you allow other sides into yours. If people choose not to speak to you, make that clear in the copy. Try too to put the story in some sort of context. Is this the first time something like this has happened?

This isn't a novelist's prose. Nor is it the kind of writing that might appear in a PhD thesis. This should be good, clear, concise English that avoids cliché. It is the bedrock of journalism. Get this right and you can approach everything else – soft news, feature writing, column writing – with greater confidence. Finally – and this applies to every piece of journalism you ever write – read it through. This is your piece. You should care about it. Does it make sense? Has it done what it set out to do? At the most basic level, are the names and addresses right? I can't tell you the number of times I have woken in the middle of the night wondering if I have put the right names in.

We started with the language of a hard-news story. Before we go to the other end of the spectrum, we should consider the 'background' news stories and 'colour pieces' that so often accompany harder stories.

These are often written to complement a hard-news story. In big murder cases, for example, papers prepare features on the defendant that are ready to run when the trial comes to an end. Thus, the day after the conviction of a notorious child murderer, the paper will run a front-page story on the court case, a 'colour piece' on the drama of the courtroom and 'backgrounders' on the life of the murderer and on his victims and their families.

The hard-news story will begin in a conventional fashion, the colour piece will begin with whatever dramatic device takes the reader into the courtroom, and the backgrounders will be written as features, in which the rules of news-story construction do not apply.

Here are some good examples from the *Daily Telegraph*, not from court, but the day after Michael Howard began to present his vision for the Conservative Party following the departure of Iain Duncan Smith as leader.

The paper's front page carried the story as its lead, written as hard news: 'Michael Howard launched the Tories on the "hard climb" back to power yesterday with a promise to lead from the centre and reunite the party's factions.

'His leadership challenge appeared unstoppable after more than half of the party's MPs backed him publicly and other potential leadership rivals confirmed that they would not stand.'

Below it came a piece by the paper's parliamentary sketch writer, Frank Johnson: 'Declaring his candidacy, Michael Howard promised: "I will lead this party from the centre." Such was the mood of amazing optimism, some of us took that worrying news surprisingly well.

'After the declaration, Andrew Marr, for the BBC, began his question by saying: "A lot of people don't know you very well."

'Mr Howard looked relieved. Until then, his problem was that a lot of people thought they knew him very well indeed. Ann Widdecombe and the liberal media had seen to that.'

And inside was a background piece on the man himself: 'Michael Howard launched his leadership campaign yesterday in the art gallery that is home to Damien Hirst's shark in formaldehyde. His critics saw it as the perfect metaphor for the politician himself – sharp, cold-blooded and dangerous.

'The man most likely to lead the Tory Party into the next election has still not quite thrown off the impression that there is, as Ann Widdecombe memorably put it, "something of the night" about him.'

As a sketch writer, Frank Johnson's task is to entertain. He is given licence to make jokes rather than to give a full account of a speech or meeting. The writer of the background piece also has greater freedom than the news reporter and can begin with whatever incident or event seems to encapsulate the spirit of the subject.

If you look through the papers you will find a number of

background pieces. They often appear alongside a story that has been making a big impact for some days, as a means of offering a new angle. Here, for example, is *The Times*, writing on a P&O cruise ship whose passengers were falling sick from a stomach bug.

'Like many passengers trapped on the cruise liner *Aurora*, the only costumes Mary Grant saw last night during the ship's Hallowe'en fancy-dress party were the crew dressed in surgical masks and gowns disinfecting her cabin.'

This is a classic way into a background piece, selecting one individual as the human face of a bigger story. It went on: 'For the past three days Mrs Grant, 66, has been confined to her cabin suffering the violent effects of the Norwalk virus, a highly contagious stomach bug that has laid low 450 passengers and crew so far.'

By now even those readers who have not followed the news story of the cruise liner can be pretty clear what is going on. The human interest way in, through the eyes of an individual, is one of the staples of journalism. You will see it after natural disasters, acts of terrorism and all other big events. It is the single Marine talking after the big battle, the Iraqi villager describing the moment the bombs began to fall, the survivor of the earthquake pointing to where her house once stood. This single human reduces the scale to something that can be understood by the reader, rendering a cataclysmic event in simple, human, emotional terms.

Once that human is established in the foreground, the writer is able to move from the individual to the crowd, from the specific to the general. Thus the *Times* report on the cruise liner moves on to doctors, company spokesmen and government officials, the figure of poor, suffering Mary Grant remaining in the mind of the reader.

We discussed earlier the basic rules of the news story. When it comes to writing these background features, the rules change. The main task here is to find a way into the story that is dramatic or otherwise enticing enough for the reader to keep going.

If you want to see it at its most professional, look at the *Daily Mail* on a Saturday, when that paper runs a series of human-interest news features, usually about the famous, often about ordinary people in extraordinary circumstances.

This, for instance, is the journalist Geoffrey Wansell, introducing a piece exploring the marriage of the footballer David Beckham and the pop singer Victoria 'Spice Girl' Adams: 'The time is well after midnight in the discreet Santo Mauro hotel in Madrid, but the sound of a man shouting at the top of his voice echoes down its elegant Art Deco corridors. The noise is disturbing, but the hotel's management is reluctant to remonstrate with its most famous resident – England's football captain, David Beckham – who has spent more than £400,000 there in the past 11 weeks.'

You feel you are there in the hotel with him, don't you? Never mind that this is probably a detail picked up from a member of staff or other guest and turned into a piece of living drama.

' "I want you here with me, Babes," Beckham is yelling at his wife Victoria on his mobile, as a member of the hotel staff approaches to ask him to be a little quieter. "You're never here. You're always in London, or with that bloke Dash in New York. We're a family. I want us to be a family." '

Here you see the full, dramatic effect of quotes as if the writer had been there noting down every word. Only the cynical would question the accuracy of the words 'with that bloke Dash in New York', which sound more like a line from a play, when the playwright is trying to introduce the characters to the audience.

In other hands – a pop paper such as the *News of the World*, for example – the story of the footballer's alleged unhappiness could have been rendered as a much more direct news story. Indeed, in the first weeks of his stay in Madrid there were a number of news stories that suggested the Beckham–Adams marriage was coming apart. But by writing it in this detailed style, the *Mail* not only conveys the impression of serious and accurate research, but also creates a more sophisticated and rounded read.

How can the paper publish direct quotes that may not actually have been made? They would justify them on the basis that they communicated the gist of what had been said. And as the words are not libellous, it is hard to see what redress the Beckhams would have.

There are other ways into background stories like these. One of the most popular is the 'they-look-like-any-normal-couple-BUT' construction, a simple solution to the problem of getting a story started. The *Mail* is good at these too. This is Natasha Courtney-Smith, writing on a woman who was raped as a fifteen-year-old girl and gave up her child for adoption.

'As they walked arm in arm along Weymouth beach last week, Pauline Simmonds and her son Trevor might have been any typical mother and son out for an afternoon stroll.'

Do you sense a 'but clause' coming? You're right: 'Only their permanent smiles and the tight hold they kept on one another betrayed the fact that this simple pleasure has been a very long time in the making.'

Yes, yes, we are getting the picture. Now tell us what the story is: 'For Pauline, the moment marked the end of an extraordinary 42-year wait to meet her firstborn son, and for Trevor, the end of a 12-year search to find his real mother. But what makes their story and its uplifting conclusion all the more amazing, is that Trevor was born after Pauline was raped as a teenager.'

Now who, after a start like that, can resist reading on?

The intro, incidentally, can become a terrible mental block for journalists. During the troubles in Northern Ireland in the 1980s, I worked with a highly experienced colleague who had developed an almost pathological fear of starting a story. This was in the days of portable typewriters rather than laptops, and he could not continue with his story until the first paragraph – or 'take' – was perfectly typed. A literal, a space in the wrong place, a change of mind would mean he had to rip out the paper and start again. Many of us find it hard to go on until we feel the intro is right. But sometimes, in the interests of meeting the deadline and of sanity, it is better to go on to do the rest of the story and come back to look again at the intro. You will be surprised how often you have written superfluous words at the start in an effort to get the piece going.

We can argue whether the examples we've been discussing are news backgrounders or features. The distinction is more important than you might imagine, for journalists tend to regard news as somehow more macho than features. This sounds like the distinction between rugby forwards and rugby backs. The former do the hard work, the latter do the showing off.

There are journalists who say rather proudly: 'I don't write features, I am a news reporter.' Similarly there are feature writers who refuse to turn out for the news pages. They may have a point, for work that appears in news pages is usually treated less delicately than feature material. News subs cannot forget that they once learned to cut from the bottom, which may have disastrous consequences for feature pieces. They also like to remove adjectives, which can leave carefully written stories stranded in a sorry no-man's-land between news and features. So in an effort to keep everyone happy, we tend to call them news features and let both sides write them.

But before we leave news, we should look at one other type of story. This is the 'soft story' or the 'funny'. These are certainly soft, but they are not always funny. Forget the WWWWW rules; the idea is to write these to entertain. In the right hands they cheer up the mood of the news pages. Done wrong, they don't.

Look out for puns. Run from punchlines you sense coming from the opening paragraph. Here is the *Mirror*, on a lavatory set up in India for a visit from the Prince of Wales. The headline, naturally, is 'Royal Flush': 'It was meant to be the ultimate royal throne. Standing in a field in a remote village, the tent might have provided the perfect stage for a Punch and Judy show.' And then comes the 'instead clause'. Yes, it's a 'modern convenience' for the Prince.

And here, from *The Times*, is a piece on a children's television character, printed in an attempt to cheer up the front page: 'Listen very carefully, children – Andy Pandy is finally clearing his throat. The longest silence in television history will end next year when the pyjama-clad puppet utters his first words.'

The only rule for these stories is that you write what you can get away with, and that will vary from paper to paper, from editor to editor. I have been hard on these examples, but there is no doubt they will have gone down a storm with many readers. This is one of the important points about journalism. There is often no absolute right or wrong, only what someone thinks is good or bad. I've often arrived for work at the *Daily Telegraph* in a furious mood over some piece of copy, only to discover that everyone at morning news conference was delighted with it.

That leaves us with features and columns. When I started, everyone wanted to be an on-the-road reporter, ideally graduating to the role of foreign 'fireman' – the reporter who gets sent abroad when the big stories break – because they seemed the most exciting and glamorous jobs in newspapers. Then more and more reporters decided they wanted to work in politics, to the point where many, including the former *Mirror* political editor Alastair Campbell, actually left journalism to become political advisers. Now there are reporters who haven't spent five minutes on a newspaper before they are expecting to be given a column. In the old days you could turn them down by explaining that they didn't have anything to say. Now they come back and point to successful columnists and claim that they don't seem to be saying much either. The truth is that there are writers who can make a seemingly mundane existence compelling and others who can render the remarkable mundane.

I cherish the memory of Richard Littlejohn, a superb, polemical columnist for the *Sun*, reacting in fury at the British Press Awards when the Columnist of the Year award was given to the *Daily Telegraph*'s Zoë Heller, who wrote each week about her life in New York. He'd had some drinks, and he was not happy. His face was red. 'How can you give Columnist of the Year to a woman who writes about a muff wax?'

It would be pointless trying to explain what makes a column, how to write a column or how to get a column. Some of the most brilliant news gatherers in the business could not write a column to save their lives, and there are writers who would not recognize a news story if it jumped on to their computer screen and wrote itself, but who turn out brilliant columns.

My only advice is to read the ones that work and try to see how they are done. At some point you may well be invited to fill in for an absent columnist. Only then will you find whether or not you can write a column that finds an audience beyond your mother.

The world of features is more open. The possibilities appear almost endless. Where is the common structure that connects features in the *Sunday Times* magazine with pieces in *Hello!* with articles in *Time Out*?

The only guide is what the newspaper or magazine you are writing for has previously run. When you have got some pieces under your belt, you can try different creative styles, but you may only be pushing your luck if you take too radical an approach in your first pieces. The history of feature writing is that writers try new approaches on imaginative magazines and papers take on these styles in slightly sanitized fashion.

There was a time, for instance, when the point of going to see a film star was to write up a rather glamorous account of his or her sexual magnetism. These were not antagonistic meetings, and the fact that the star might be feeling out of sorts was not dwelt upon. A fifteen-minute talk – one of a series organized in a hotel suite for British journalists – might be presented as a lengthy, intimate conversation.

Then the clever journalist Lynn Barber developed a reputation for turning not only the interview but also everything around the interview into copy. So, enthralled, we read of difficulties with PRs, arguments with celebrities, even of the trouble Ms Barber had encountered in getting to the interview. This was terrific stuff, but had the sorry effect of making too many lesser talents think they could do the same. It is always a good idea to use 'I' sparingly in newspapers. Unless you have made a big reputation for yourself, you might remember that we are more interested in reading about the person you have come to see than about you.

Again, the way to learn is to read as much as you can. See how good feature writers use the material that is in front of them. See how they take whatever colour, information or references are to be had from other places. There's a lot more to this than merely sticking a few adjectives on news copy. Nothing brings the reader down faster than a string of clichés. The best feature writers use skills of pacing, chronology and drama. They know when to explain what is happening and when to let their characters do the explaining for them. They make quotes work for their space on the page. Underpinning all these tricks, however, are the basics of journalism: an ear for a quote, an eye for telling detail, the sense that there is drama to be brought out.

The late Sir David English, the man who created the modern *Daily Mail* when he changed its format from broadsheet to tabloid, used to talk about the importance of contrast in papers. 'Light and shade! Light and shade!' he instructed.

He knew that it wasn't enough to offer hard news on page after page. There had to be humour, glamour and even whimsy. The paper's critics accuse it of following a predictable formula, but there is a variety of stories in the *Mail*, from hard news to whimsical features. If you look for some connection between these diverse pieces you can find it only in the professionalism with which each is produced. You may not want to read certain stories, but someone will.

The important thing is to read everything, to see how others do it. You may not want to write the same way, but it is helpful to learn the tricks. Whether you are producing a tight news story or a 10,000-word feature for a magazine, you are writing to be read. Kick out the clichés, keep down the journalese and aim high.

My Big Break I

John Carlin, foreign correspondent, the *Observer*

'I was working in Argentina on the English-language *Buenos Aires Herald* on 2 April 1982. This was my first job in journalism. I had been at the paper six months, writing about theatre, film, football and disappeared people. 2 April 1982 was the date the Falklands War broke out.'

Charlie Catchpole, television critic, *Daily Express* and *Daily Star*

'I was caption-writing on the London *Evening Standard* when I went with a colleague for a drink in the bar at London Weekend Television, where I met two executives of ITV Sport who mentioned that Brian Moore – then ITV's number one football commentator – was unhappy with his contract and might join the BBC. I filed the story and ITV immediately improved Moore's contract. Moore phoned me to thank me, and I was offered a job as a reporter on the paper's TV/show business beat.'

Paul Rees, editor, *Q* magazine

'Getting a staff job on the West Midlands' entertainment monthly *Brum Beat*. My appointment doubled the number of full-time staff on the title at a stroke. For the princely sum of £50 per week I wrote and subbed copy, did flatplans, sold all advertising for the title (as a free publication this was what kept it afloat), answered the phones and did everything else required by the editor. In the process I got a thorough background in the mechanics of putting a magazine together, but an equally invaluable education as to the level of passion required to do so.'

PART 2

THE ISSUES

7

The straight and narrow path

We hear a great deal about the freedom of the press, but it is a freedom that only goes so far. British papers may indeed be free from interference – only newspaper proprietors get to tell editors what to publish – but that doesn't mean they are free to print what they like. Some pieces will get papers into nothing but trouble: trouble with the criminal law, trouble with the civil courts or trouble with the Press Complaints Commission. If you are not careful, those pieces could be written by you.

To try to stop you getting into trouble, newspapers have lawyers. Their job is to read pieces before publication to check that a story isn't breaking the law, or libelling someone, or breaching the rules of the Press Complaints Commission. But lawyers are at the end of the chain – and you are unlikely to find one in a local newspaper or magazine office. Commissioning editors may have some knowledge of how you can and can't behave and what you should and shouldn't write. News editors make it their business to know. So should you.

So, what kind of stories lead you into contentious territory? Almost anything can, however innocently intended. The danger areas are clear. Most of them are covered in the code of conduct of the Press Complaints Commission.

The Commission is the newspaper industry's main line of defence against the continuing threat of government legislation on press conduct. Every time a newspaper behaves in a way that politicians do not like, there is a demand for new laws to curb the press. You may not be surprised to hear that such demands come loudest from politicians who have been caught with their trousers down.

You might think that the bare-legged ones would explain to their voters why they choose to abandon their spouses and spend the evening enjoying the discipline of a top dominatrix in a West End brothel: they prefer to attack the messenger – that's us journalists – on the basis that what they get up to is no one's business but their own. Almost invariably, the next step is to denounce press intrusion and to revere the concept of personal privacy. Then they finish the job by calling for new laws on newspaper regulation to end the former and protect the latter.

But let us be fair: some politicians make clear where they stand on the press before they get into trouble. A good example is David Mellor, who as Culture Secretary back in 1988 accused newspapers of behaving in an outrageous fashion. We were drinking, he said, in the 'Last Chance Saloon'. In other words, if we didn't improve our behaviour, there would be new laws to make us do so.

The Conservative government – which was to become mired in accusations of sleaze and sex scandal – set up an inquiry into the press, led by Lord Calcutt. In January 1991, as a result of his recommendations, the Press Complaints Commission came into being, the latest attempt at industry self-regulation. Newspapers pay for the PCC, which acts as a watchdog on standards on behalf of the public. As long as the PCC is seen to work, then newspapers believe they can stave off legislation. Governments, for their part, continue to dislike the newspaper industry, but would prefer not to have to tackle it head on: confronting it is the kind of thing that gets a politician a bad press.

I explained that Mr Mellor spoke out before there was any hint of trouble. He did, but the Last Chance Saloon was not the last we heard of him. Four years later, he found himself starring in the kind of headlines he detested, when it was revealed that he had been cheating on his wife with an actress. The press had got its revenge.

So the PCC Code of Conduct is fundamental to the way newspapers behave. Some of its rules are an extension of existing laws; others, such as attitudes to privacy, in effect anticipate the way in which the law – especially European law – is heading.

In the words of the PCC:

> All members of the press have a duty to maintain the highest professional standards. This Code sets the benchmark for those ethical standards, protecting both the rights of the individual and the public's right to know. It is the cornerstone of the system of self-regulation to which the industry has made a binding commitment . . .
>
> It is the responsibility of editors and publishers to implement the Code and they should take care to ensure it is observed rigorously by all editorial staff and external contributors, including non-journalists, in printed and online versions of publications.

It is worth remembering that second paragraph. There is much mischief still to be made in journalism, but some of the stunts reporters used to pull to get stories would now result in disciplinary action. My friend the *Mail on Sunday* reporter who bluffed her way into a hospital by borrowing a white coat and posing as a doctor would be in big trouble today. Be aware that news desks may turn a blind eye to the techniques you use and may even encourage you to bend the rules to get a story. However, once you go beyond the Code, trouble is likely to follow. You may think you were being egged on to do what you did, but if the PCC decides you went too far, you can expect to find yourself on your own. You will probably find it a term of any contract with a newspaper that you work within the rules of the PCC and if you are caught breaking the rules, don't expect anyone on the paper to admit asking you to do so.

For the Code to work, papers need to abide as much by the spirit as by the letter of it. In practice, they work extremely hard to find reasons why their stories fall the right side of the rules. The Code needs to balance the rights of the individual with what is in the public interest to be published. So, naturally, papers try to define the public interest as widely as possible. Newspapers must cooperate swiftly and fully with the PCC. If they are censured, they must print the finding of the Commission in full and with some prominence.

And so to the Code itself:

1 *Accuracy*
   i) The Press must take care not to publish inaccurate, misleading or distorted information, including pictures.
   ii) A significant inaccuracy, misleading statement or distortion once recognized must be corrected, promptly and with due prominence, and – where appropriate – an apology published.
   iii) The Press, whilst free to be partisan, must distinguish clearly between comment, conjecture and fact.
   iv) A publication must report fairly and accurately the outcome of an action for defamation to which it has been a party, unless an agreed settlement states otherwise, or an agreed statement is published.

2 *Opportunity to reply*
   A fair opportunity for reply to inaccuracies must be given when reasonably called for.

This seems pretty uncontroversial, but you can imagine the arguments differentiating comment and fact and accuracy and inaccuracy. A reluctance to acknowledge, let alone apologize for, mistakes has become ingrained in newspapers. They prefer to imply infallibility, despite all the evidence to the contrary. Generations of reporters have been brought up to avoid printing a correction at all costs.

The Guardian has developed a more efficient means of dealing with the problem: a daily section in the paper corrects mistakes notified to it, often without intervention from readers. A readers' editor rules on what should be corrected. The paper believes that a willingness to admit its mistakes adds to rather than detracts from a reputation for accuracy. The paper is right, but only the *Independent on Sunday* and the *Mirror* have followed its example. The *Guardian*'s approach has enhanced the paper's reputation. The corrections and clarifications column is one of the most popular in the newspaper and has prompted the paper to publish anthologies of the strangest.

3 *Privacy[1]

  i) Everyone is entitled to respect for his or her private and family life, home, health and correspondence, including digital communications. Editors will be expected to justify intrusions into any individual's private life without consent.

  ii) It is unacceptable to photograph individuals in private places without their consent.

  Note – Private places are public or private property where there is a reasonable expectation of privacy.

This is one of the most contentious areas of journalism: what is private and what is public? It is also an increasingly difficult area of law. Until recently in Britain, we had very little legal right to privacy. Then with the passing into British law of the European Convention on Human Rights, we had the beginnings of such law. The problem is that the Convention seeks to protect both privacy, under Article 8, and freedom of expression, under Article 10.

How do you weigh up these competing rights?

Take, for instance, that essential element in the popular Sunday newspaper genre, the kiss-and-tell story. I may regard my drunken night of shame with the silicone-breasted lap dancer as a private matter that a newspaper has no right to publish. The lap dancer may regard it as a principle of free expression that she can tell the world about it.

The short answer is that judges are likely to develop the rules as we go along, case by case. In 2001, Lord Woolf delivered a judgment in the Court of Appeal that had journalists cheering when he overturned an injunction that the Premier League footballer Gary Flitcroft had obtained to prevent the *Sunday People* writing about an extramarital affair. The cheering came not so much because journalists

---

[1] See page 119 for explanation of asterisk.

wanted to write about footballers' affairs. Most don't. But the Woolf judgment enshrined an important principle of press freedom. The Flitcroft injunction related to a low-rent sex story. But what if it had been obtained by a hypocritical politician, with power over people's lives?

Lord Woolf wrote: 'A public figure is entitled to a private life. The individual, however, should recognize that because of his public position he must expect and accept that his or her actions will be more closely scrutinized by the media. Even trivial facts relating to a public figure can be of great interest to readers and other observers of the media. Conduct which in the case of a private individual would be the appropriate subject of comment can be the proper subject of comment in the case of a public figure.'

That sounds promising for newspapers, but this is an area of some uncertainty. Even the parts of the PCC Code that appear clear offer complications once you read them closely. No long-lens photography into private places. But what is a private place? It is a public or private property 'where there is a reasonable expectation of privacy'. Once again, we are in areas of interpretation. A private property sounds pretty clear. But what if the property is overlooked by a public road? Would what goes on in sight of that road necessarily be private? If the householder knows that his property is overlooked, does that give him a reasonable expectation of privacy? And what if the area in question is a hotel pool, one of the most popular hunting grounds for patrolling paparazzi? If the PCC decided that all pool shots were now in contravention of the Code, what would the popular press find to publish?

In a ruling that may have serious implications for papers, the PCC decided that a local newspaper had infringed the code when it took a picture inside a café to illustrate a restaurant review. A customer who appeared in the photograph complained that it had been taken without his permission. The newspaper argued that the café was in effect a public place, because any member of the public could walk in.

The PCC disagreed: 'Customers of a quiet café could expect to sit inside such an establishment without having to worry that surreptitious photographs would be taken of them and published in newspapers. There was no suggestion that the complainant was easily visible from the street and the Commission considered that all the circumstances suggested that he and his companion were clearly in a place where they had a reasonable expectation of privacy.'

In another controversial case, however, the PCC declined to uphold a complaint by the television presenter Anna Ford, who was pictured in the *Daily Mail* walking in a bikini on a beach with her boyfriend. The beach was public, but couldn't she expect privacy? The PCC said not, and Ms Ford failed in her attempt to challenge the decision in the High Court. She told the BBC afterwards: 'It was the press which took secretive photographs and sold them for profit who were the intrusion into our privacy. Any citizen has the right to privacy on a quiet beach anywhere in the world if they are seeking privacy.'

So the editor of the *Mail* was guilty of a lack of gallantry, but not of breaching the PCC rules. In another case, involving the disc jockey Sarah Cox, the *People* published pictures of her and her husband on honeymoon. They were outside their private beach cabin, but visible through long lenses from the Indian Ocean. The PCC declined to adjudicate, because the *People* published a full apology. The couple then sued the paper and won £50,000 in damages in an out-of-court settlement. The case wasn't actually heard, so created no legal precedent on privacy. But it encouraged those in the public eye to use the law rather than the PCC.

There is another point to note here, which is the presence of that little asterisk by the Code entry. There is a get-out to all these rules, which is that what you were doing was in the 'public interest'. We will examine the public interest more closely. For the moment, let's just remember that it is probably something different from what the public finds interesting.

4 *Harassment
- i) Journalists must not engage in intimidation, harassment or persistent pursuit.
- ii) They must not persist in questioning, telephoning, pursuing or photographing individuals once asked to desist; nor remain on their property when asked to leave and must not follow them.
- iii) Editors must ensure these principles are observed by those working for them and take care not to use non-compliant material from other sources.

When does persistence become harassment? These are hard lines to draw. I cannot think of a news editor who, on being told by a member of his staff that someone does not want to speak, would not instruct the reporter to go back and try again. News editors learn to issue that order as soon as they sit in the chair. Ask a door-to-door salesman how much commission he would make if he took no for an answer every time he rang a doorbell. The principles are not very different.

Much depends on the circumstances – and, once again, there is the matter of public interest. It is one thing to keep knocking at the door of a woman whose child has been murdered, quite another to badger a man to whom you want to put accusations of criminal activity.

In the case of the latter, the public – and the PCC – would probably accept your right to keep on asking. In the case of the former, you are heading for trouble.

But you wouldn't do it in the case of the former? You might be surprised how many would, urged on by a news desk eager for the first talk. The 'doorstep', the uninvited appearance of a reporter at the door of someone involved in a story, is one of the set pieces of journalism. There are reporters who will plead, cajole or threaten, who will shout through letterboxes and push notes offering money under the door, who will pose as council officials or follow other visitors straight into the house.

Which brings us to:

5 *Intrusion into grief or shock*
  In cases involving personal grief or shock, inquiries and approaches
  must be made with sympathy and discretion and publication handled sensitively. This should not restrict the right to report legal
  proceedings, such as inquests.

If you ever work on a local newspaper you will certainly find
yourself standing on a doorstep one morning waiting to try to speak
to a woman who has just learned that her husband has been killed
in a road accident. Or, grimmer still, to the parent of a dead child.

How would you feel if you were in their shoes? Some react with
anger and chase you from the door in a fury. Some are polite, and
don't actually threaten you as they ask you to leave. If things go
well, you might get a few words. And, remarkably often, you find
yourself invited in for a long, moving talk with a spouse or parent
who finds it helpful to talk about what has happened and who
wants some public record of a loved one's death. They sit you down
and make you a cup of tea and bring out the photo album and let
you borrow a couple of pictures to put in the paper. And then you
are out of the house, clutching the snaps, knowing you have got a
good story and a by-line to look forward to and trying not to think
about what *they* have got to look forward to.

Some reporters love this kind of work and are very good at it.
Others handle it with such insensitivity that they do nothing but
give journalism a bad name. These days, particularly in deaths
involving crime, police often step in to help grieving families. They
may try to negotiate a deal with reporters that, in return for a
statement from the family, the press will avoid approaching them.
Some feel there should actually be laws that prevent the press
intruding into grief in this manner, but I believe that any such law
would set a dangerous precedent. People may not wish to talk, but
we should be free to ask. That must be our right in an open and
free society. In any case, there are people who are clearly prepared
to talk and who may indeed *want* to talk in order to publicize some
perceived wrong.

There is another area where great sensitivities are also involved, but where it is important that reporters assert their right to publish details that may cause distress. One of the important functions of newspapers is to report legal proceedings. The editor may decide that there are elements of a case that can be left out, but you should not allow a distressed relative to persuade you that the details of a coroner's inquest or a court case are so unpleasant that they should go unreported.

In a situation such as this, you must stand your ground. It is for the editor to decide what should and should not be reported. Your only obligation is to report accurately, and in doing that, you are likely to report sensitively too.

6 *Children

    i) Young people should be free to complete their time at school without unnecessary intrusion.

    ii) A child under 16 must not be interviewed or photographed on issues involving their own or another child's welfare unless a custodial parent or similarly responsible adult consents.

    iii) Pupils must not be approached or photographed at school without the permission of the school authorities.

    iv) Minors must not be paid for material involving children's welfare, nor parents or guardians for material about their children or wards, unless it is clearly in the child's interest.

    v) Editors must not use the fame, notoriety or position of a parent or guardian as sole justification for publishing details of a child's private life

Think carefully before doing any reporting involving children. It is easy to fall foul of the rules even in something as innocent as a *vox pop*. You might think it is entirely reasonable to ask those children sitting by themselves in the corner of McDonald's how much fast food they eat in a week. When their parents see the pictures and comments in the paper, they may claim that you have breached the PCC guidelines in talking to their children about matters of welfare without their parents' consent and that you have implied that the children are not following a proper diet. So make sure a parent or a teacher knows what you are doing and has given consent.

There are, on the other hand, times when you are entitled to make use of that public interest defence. Very often, you are not going to get children to talk about drugs, crime, sex or other things they get up to by asking their parents first. It is in the public interest to hear the authentic voice of alienated youth. In other words, if you have managed to get a gang of children sniffing glue on derelict land to talk about their lives, you should be in the clear, parents' permission or no parents' permission.

But beware children who talk themselves up. The little gangster whose life you report may have made things up. The fact that he has made himself look like a tearaway may not help when his parents complain to the PCC on the basis that you had no right to talk to him.

Then there are the children of the famous, a continual source of confusion and debate. There are thousands of under eighteens we might find taking drugs, shoplifting or smashing bus shelters. It is only when they are the children of the famous that they become a story. But should the son of a television presenter find himself reported just because of his famous parent? Is a drugs case involving a politician's daughter different from a case involving the daughter of a plumber? More interesting, certainly. But more in the public interest?

When the *News of the World* reported that Prince Harry, then sixteen, had been drinking heavily and smoking marijuana, there was general agreement that it was a matter of public interest. Similarly, when Euan Blair, oldest son of Tony Blair, was picked up drunk in Leicester Square, Downing Street accepted that the matter was of legitimate public interest. If the boy had been drunk at a private party, there might have been a different argument, but this episode had occurred in a public place. Certainly Mr Blair was quick to complain to the PCC about other stories involving his children, including one that Euan had applied to Oxford University.

His name appeared on lists of candidates on a noticeboard in a college, but the *Daily Telegraph* was criticized by the PCC for reporting the matter. On other occasions, Downing Street tried to prevent papers from publishing pictures of the Blairs' youngest child, Leo. Newspapers complained that Tony Blair had often talked about his children and that as he had in effect put them in the public domain, it was wrong to try to prevent their activities being reported.

This is an area where it seems impossible to find a consensus, and editors will make their decisions on the basis of the importance of the story, the principle involved and the risk attached. For your part, you need to be aware of the trouble that this area can involve.

7 **Children in sex cases*
    i) The press must not, even if legally free to do so, identify children under 16 who are victims or witnesses in cases involving sex offences.
    ii) In any press report of a case involving a sexual offence against a child –
        i) The child must not be identified.
        ii) The adult may be identified.
        iii) The word 'incest' must not be used where a child victim might be identified.
        iv) Care must be taken that nothing in the report implies the relationship between the accused and the child.

8 **Hospitals*
    i) Journalists must identify themselves and obtain permission from a responsible executive before entering non-public areas of hospitals or similar institutions to pursue inquiries.
    ii) The restrictions on intruding into privacy are particularly relevant to inquiries about individuals in hospitals or similar institutions.

I mentioned my friend from the *Mail on Sunday* earlier. Hospitals really do take this kind of thing seriously. So, now, do papers.

9 *Reporting of crime*
  i) Relatives or friends of persons convicted or accused of crime should not generally be identified without their consent, unless they are genuinely relevant to the story.
  ii) Particular regard should be paid to the potentially vulnerable position of children who witness, or are victims of, crime. This should not restrict the right to report legal proceedings.

10 **Clandestine devices and subterfuge*
  i) The press must not seek to obtain or publish material acquired by using hidden cameras or clandestine listening devices; or by intercepting private or mobile telephone calls, messages or emails; or by the unauthorized removal of documents or photographs.
  ii) Engaging in misrepresentation or subterfuge can generally be justified only in the public interest and then only when the material cannot be obtained by other means.

We can have all kinds of arguments over the nature of 'clandestine'. Many people – not least the Prince of Wales, whose telephone conversations with his mistress Camilla Parker Bowles were recorded and printed – have been embarrassed by reporting of phone calls. Again, there is that public interest defence. If this is the only way to get material that it is in the public interest to publish, then there is a justification. You might ask what you are doing using this kind of technical gear if the story isn't in the public interest

Thank heavens for that asterisk. How far would *News of the World* investigations get if its reporters could not pose as gangsters, drug dealers, businessmen and every other character they assume in order to trap their targets into confessing criminal activity? But note that, while you are not meant to use misrepresentation or subterfuge, the Code does not demand that you actually identify yourself as a journalist in every situation.

To take a trivial example: if you stop at some roadblock without saying who you are to ask a policeman what is going on and he chooses to tell you, you have done nothing wrong. If you stop at a roadblock and pretend to be another police officer, you are using subterfuge. People are often outraged that journalists can use information they have picked up without identifying themselves as journalists. To which there is a simple reply: tough.

11 *Victims of sexual assault*
The press must not identify victims of sexual assault or publish material likely to contribute to such identification unless there is adequate justification and they are legally free to do so.

12 *Discrimination*
   i) The press must avoid prejudicial or pejorative reference to an individual's race, colour, religion, sex, sexual orientation or to any physical or mental illness or disability.
   ii) Details of an individual's race, colour, religion, sexual orientation, physical or mental illness or disability must be avoided unless genuinely relevant to the story.

Here's another potential minefield. The generation of sub-editors who thought that Irishness was synonymous with stupidity has retired, but there are still a lot of reporters and subs around who can't put a picture of a woman in the paper without wanting to find a pun to do with her breasts.

The identification of muggers and other criminals as 'black' has long been contentious, on the basis that it encourages unhelpful racial stereotyping. On the other hand, it is a factual description in an area where identification is an issue. Nowadays, papers tend to report the colour of skin of suspects whatever it is, which has the merit of equality.

13 *Financial journalism*
   i) Even where the law does not prohibit it, journalists must not use for their own profit financial information they receive in advance of its general publication, nor should they pass such information to others.
   ii) They must not write about shares or securities in whose performance they know that they or their close families have a significant

financial interest without disclosing the interest to the editor or financial editor.

iii) They must not buy or sell, either directly or through nominees or agents, shares or securities about which they have written recently or about which they intend to write in the near future.

The former *Mirror* editor Piers Morgan breached the Code in 2000 when it was discovered that he and other journalists at the paper had bought shares tipped in the City Slickers column, written by Anil Bhoyrul and James Hipwell. The two City journalists left the *Mirror*. Mr Morgan did not, or not then, anyway. He left four years later, after taking the decision to publish pictures purporting to show British Army torture in Iraq that were later found to be fake.

14 *Confidential sources*
Journalists have a moral obligation to protect confidential sources of information.

Would you go to prison to protect yours? Note that the obligation is moral rather than legal, but your reputation in the profession will plummet if you reveal sources that you promised to keep confidential.

The kind of pressure that may be exerted on journalists was seen in 2002 during the inquiry by Lord Saville into Bloody Sunday, the day in 1972 when a civil rights march in Londonderry ended with thirteen people shot dead by British paratroopers.

In the late 1990s, the *Daily Telegraph* reporter Toby Harnden had interviewed some of the former paratroopers involved in the shooting. Two television reporters had also interviewed soldiers for a Channel 4 documentary on the twenty-fifth anniversary of the shooting. The journalists were called before the Saville Inquiry and instructed to hand over their notes and identify the soldiers they had interviewed.

On the basis that they had promised the soldiers anonymity before interviewing them, the journalists refused. They were all threatened with imprisonment, a threat that hung over them for many months during an inquiry estimated to have cost some £155 million. On the day he took final evidence, in 2004, Lord Saville announced that he would not pursue the journalists.

'The way I have been pursued and vilified by the tribunal for maintaining my journalistic duty to protect confidential sources is a disgrace and Lord Saville should be ashamed over how he dealt with this issue,' Mr Harnden said afterwards.

Unfortunately, journalistic duty tends to impress journalists more than courts. You may find yourself in contempt of court for refusing to say who gave you certain information. But cheer up. If – as has happened from time to time – you are committed to prison for a little while, you know you will emerge as a hero of the newspaper business, though whether the rest of the population admires you is questionable There is a danger that you will merely be seen as obstructing lawful inquiries. When it comes to being a hero, the journalist has got to fancy his or her chances over the judge, not least because colleagues in the press will write that a noble cause is served.

15 *Witness payments in criminal trials*
  i) No payment or offer of payment to a witness – or any person who may reasonably be expected to be called as a witness – should be made in any case once proceedings are active as defined by the Contempt of Court Act 1981.
  ii) This prohibition lasts until the suspect has been freed unconditionally by police without charge or bail or the proceedings are otherwise discontinued; or has entered a guilty plea to the court; or, in the event of a not guilty plea, the court has announced its verdict.
  iii) *Where proceedings are not yet active but are likely and foreseeable, editors must not make or offer payment to any person who may reasonably be expected to be called as a witness, unless the information concerned ought demonstrably to be published in the public interest and there is an overriding need to make or promise payment for this to be done; and all reasonable steps have been taken to ensure no financial dealings

influence the evidence those witnesses give. In no circumstances should such payment be conditional on the outcome of a trial.

iv) Any payment or offer of payment made to a person later cited to give evidence in proceedings must be disclosed to the prosecution and defence. The witness must be advised of this requirement.

Newspapers have been paying witnesses for years, to secure colourful background pieces on big crimes. There is a danger, however, that doing deals before a trial may affect the evidence that such witnesses give. The *Sunday Telegraph* got into big trouble in 1980, when it emerged that it proposed to pay one of the prosecution witnesses in the trial of the former Liberal leader Jeremy Thorpe. The deal was that he received more money if a conviction was secured, which created a financial incentive to tailor his evidence. You will see that the PCC rule makes a special point of forbidding the making of payments that are conditional on the outcome of the trial.

More recently, other payments to witnesses have caused concern. When you pay someone to come forward with claims that a pop star had unlawful sex with them years before, can you be sure that you are getting a true story, rather than an inflated account designed to make money? The risk is yours. If you have made a deal with someone involved in a criminal trial, is there a danger that he or she will keep back important evidence to make the after-trial story more exciting?

The Labour government contemplated making it a criminal offence to offer money to witnesses, but backed off, preferring to leave the matter with self-regulation and the PCC. Journalists divided at the time, some suggesting that it was never necessary to offer payment, given that all relevant information was likely to come out at the trial. Others argued that there was a public interest in witnesses putting as much information as they had into the public domain and that if it took a financial incentive to encourage them to do so, that was a reasonable price to pay.

On the basis that the less government interferes with the press the better, I was pleased by the decision to leave matters with self-regulation. It would surely be wrong to prevent witnesses telling their story at any point. And once you accept that they should be allowed to talk, it is hard to justify preventing them from benefiting by doing so. This is an area where it pays to exercise some care. Activity that may just seem enthusiastic to you may take on a different complexion when it is presented by an angry barrister in a court of law, seeking to have the judge throw out a witness's evidence on the basis he has been talking to the press.

16 *Payment to criminals*
  i) Payment or offers of payment for stories, pictures or information, which seek to exploit a particular crime or to glorify or glamorize crime in general, must not be made directly or via agents to convicted or confessed criminals or to their associates – who may include family, friends and colleagues.
  ii) Editors invoking the public interest to justify payment or offers would need to demonstrate that there was good reason to believe the public interest would be served. If, despite payment, no public interest emerged, then the material should not be published.

Here's another part of the Code that causes much anguish. In the past, papers have been eager to print the life stories of armed robbers or pay the spouses of murderers for their testimony. Their willingness to pay for such accounts has often incensed relatives of the victims of their crimes.

But if the purpose of the rule is generally seen to be good, its application causes confusion. The *Guardian* was furious to be censured for paying a life prisoner, who wrote a weekly diary on prison life, for his account of the writer and Conservative peer Jeffrey Archer in gaol. Yet the *Daily Mail* escaped criticism for serializing the peer's own account of his life inside, apparently because the money went to a charity. Yet it was arguable that Lord Archer benefited from the attendant publicity for his book.

The *Guardian* argued that its prisoner's account was in the public interest, in throwing light on conditions inside. The PCC decided it was not.

In 2003, the *Mirror* signed up the farmer Tony Martin, who had become a national figure after he was convicted of manslaughter for shooting dead a fleeing burglar. The *Mirror* argued that there had been such interest in the rights and wrongs of Mr Martin's conviction that his personal account was in the public interest. The argument succeeded.

So what exactly is the public interest? The Press Complaints Commission explains it, and how we might interpret it, like this:

1. The public interest includes, but is not confined to:
    i) Detecting or exposing crime or serious impropriety.
    ii) Protecting public health and safety.
    iii) Preventing the public from being misled by an action or statement of an individual or organization.
2. There is a public interest in freedom of expression itself.
3. Whenever the public interest is invoked, the PCC will require editors to demonstrate fully how the public interest was served.
4. The PCC will consider the extent to which material is already in the public domain, or will become so.
5. In cases involving children under 16, editors must demonstrate an exceptional public interest to override the normally paramount interest of the child.

You will notice that the PCC uses the term 'includes'. It is up to you to justify contentious work on the basis that it is in the public interest. It is a common observation that the public interest is different from what the public find interesting – so common that I made it earlier in this piece. So gossip about a pop star or a politician may be hugely interesting to many members of the public, but it is not necessarily in the public interest to spread it.

But just when we are getting used to working on that basis, along comes a British judge to suggest that the public interest and what interests the public may at times be almost synonymous. Here is more of Lord Woolf, in the judgment about the Blackburn Rovers Gary Flitcroft which we talked about earlier:

> In many of these situations it would be overstating the position to say there is a public interest in the information being published. It would be more accurate to say that the public have an understandable and so a legitimate interest in being told the information ... The courts must not ignore the fact that if newspapers do not publish information which the public are interested in, there will be fewer newspapers published, which will not be in the public interest.

Those words are as encouraging as any you will find from a judge on the right of papers to publish what their readers might want to read. It is in the public interest that more newspapers are published, and it takes a certain kind of story to stimulate the public to read. This is as good as it gets from British judges. Let us tiptoe away now, before he changes his mind.

That was a stroll around what you might call the industry's own rules. What of the law? There is enough in this subject for a separate book, and if you are serious about writing stories, it's worth buying one. In legal territory a little learning really is a dangerous thing. While news departments of newspapers are attuned to the nuances of the law, features editors often aren't. It is helpful for you to have an idea of the trouble you could be getting into. So here, in broadest brush-strokes, are some of the perils you should bear in mind.

Firstly, you should remember that, as a journalist, you have no special privileges under the law. The police might allow you a little closer to the crime scene on production of your press card, but only if they want to. You can knock on doors, but no one is obliged to open them. And when you smuggle that replica gun into the airport to prove the inadequacy of security, don't think that calling yourself a journalist will protect you from being thrown into a cell. Nor will it protect you from being charged, if you have committed an offence. Secondly, you need to worry not only about the criminal, but also about the civil law. In other words, your work could not only put you in prison but also cost your paper several thousand pounds' worth of damages.

Finally, the relationship between the press and the law works both ways. There are areas where the law is clearly defined and you would be foolish to break it. But it is a mistake to assume that the police, court officials and judges are always right. Newspapers have reporting rights on behalf of the public. They are part of the mechanism that ensures that justice is seen to be done. However, there are many judges, lawyers and clients who would prefer to keep all kinds of things out of the papers and will happily ignore reporting rights to do so. Newspapers spend much time and money challenging occasions on which they are forbidden from reporting or identifying parties in court cases. Often, they win.

There are many ways in which you can fall foul of the criminal or civil law, some of which may never have crossed your mind. Your report of the racist comments made by a member of the British National Party may break the law in the same way that he has; your hard-hitting column on asylum seekers could result in an interview with police; the company memo given to you by a whistle-blower could result in the whistle-blower, you and your paper ending up in court for breach of confidence. This is an expanding area of the civil law that is increasingly used as an alternative means of achieving privacy.

Where, for instance, a newspaper plans to print a nanny's inside story of life with a famous family, it may be prevented from doing so on the basis that this would be a breach of confidence. You, as the writer, your newspaper and the nanny would all be in breach. Lawyers, however, make the point that 'there is no confidence in iniquity'. In other words, the person you are writing about cannot use the law of confidence to stop you revealing something as a wrongdoing.

Or, in reporting the contents of an interesting internal Civil Service memo, you may find yourself liable for breach of copyright, the copyright belonging to the person who wrote the memo, or to the government department on whose behalf it was written.

Hardly a day goes by in any newsroom without one or more legal questions coming up. The two you will face most often are contempt of court and libel.

CONTEMPT OF COURT

Contempt covers a lot of ground, from refusing to do something a court says – like giving the Saville Inquiry the names of former paratroopers interviewed about Bloody Sunday – to interfering in a court process, perhaps by publishing information that has not been discussed in court. If you publish background details of a crime while the case is going through court, for instance, you may be in contempt. The reason is that a jury is supposed to decide a case on the basis of the information put before it, not on extraneous detail gleaned from a newspaper report.

That is why newspapers wait until the end of a case before printing background interviews with relatives or witnesses. After murder trials, you will often read interviews with people describing life with the murderer. These people may have had no involvement in the court case because their account of the criminal's violent past had no legal relevance, but if the newspaper had printed their accounts during the trial it might have affected the view of the jury.

Most papers are aware of their responsibilities in this area, but sometimes stories get through that shouldn't. In 2002, a court ordered a retrial of a group of professional footballers accused of serious assaults. While the jury was still considering its verdict, the *Sunday Mirror* printed an interview with the father of the victim, which condemned the footballers in outspoken terms. The case was abandoned, and the editor called before the court to explain his lapse.

These rules mean that there are in effect two periods during which you are pretty much free to report what you like: before proceedings are 'active' and once they have finished. So, for instance, in the aftermath of a crime, you may carry the most graphic descriptions of the event, quoting witnesses at length and describing in detail what the criminals did. You can speculate on their motive, wonder how they had planned the crime and link them to previous ones. All that changes once police have arrested someone.

Once proceedings are active, all discussion of the crime ceases until it comes to trial. And at the trial you must confine yourself to what is said in court. In the weeks or months before trial, those charged will appear in magistrates' courts for remand or committal hearings – these are the preliminary hearings before the main case is heard – at which point you can report only the barest details: essentially their name, age and address and whether they respond to the charge.

During the case itself, you can report what is said in court, unless discussions take place without the jury. These are sessions you are usually restricted from reporting. Your reports should be an accurate and fair summary of the court proceedings, though just as barristers dramatize their evidence, so you can select the most newsworthy bits, provided that the source of your material is the courtroom. You can also 'sketch' the proceedings, which is a colourful account of the dramatic scene. In doing so, you must be careful that you do not imply the guilt or innocence of the defendant, or write anything that the jurors could not have observed for themselves.

Once the case is over, you can return to the dramatic stuff. This is when the most lurid pieces in newspapers appear. Some of them may be highly exaggerated, but as there is no longer a jury to worry about, there are no worries about contempt of court.

What does 'active' mean? There is legal confusion about this, with the law since 1981 being that proceedings are active once someone has been arrested. But police and journalists traditionally used to work on the basis that proceedings become active once someone has been charged.

In most criminal inquiries there is a helpful, if mutually suspicious, relationship between police and press. The police need the press to give publicity to the investigation, so that witnesses may come forward. But if too much detail emerges – how, for instance, a murder victim died – the inquiry might be compromised.

In practice, newspapers will report a murder inquiry in great detail, including whatever information the police may give them about a suspect to keep the story in the public eye. Once a suspect is arrested, papers can publish only the barest details. In the days when proceedings became 'active' when a suspect was charged, there often used to be unofficial cooperation between police and press to the point where police appeared to delay charging suspects until after the papers had 'gone to bed'. That meant that papers could print detail about arrests because proceedings were not 'active'. The police were happy because their arrest received good publicity. The papers were happy because they had a proper story. And if the suspect happened to have been charged by the time the papers hit the streets, well, that wasn't their fault, was it?

Whenever there is a big murder story, there is almost invariably concern about the reporting of the eventual arrest, with lawyers suggesting that a fair trial is being put in jeopardy. I was in Sheffield the night South Yorkshire Police caught, quite by chance, Peter Sutcliffe, a serial murder who had become known as the Yorkshire Ripper.

The excitement among South Yorkshire Police – the Ripper had been operating in the area controlled by their West Yorkshire neighbours, who had failed to nail him over several years – left no one in any doubt that they had the right man. They even put up the arresting officers at a press conference. In theory, with Sutcliffe charged, newspapers were in contempt in the way they covered the arrest. But this was one of those times when nothing was going to hold them back, especially after the encouragement offered by the police.

There are other occasions when, as a result of the publicity given to a manhunt, it would be impossible to expect papers to say nothing once a suspect has been arrested. If the public has been gripped for a week by the search for a wanted man, they are entitled to know that he has been arrested. A small paragraph in the paper would meet legal requirements, but in practice no one expresses concern when papers work such an arrest into a front-page story.

LIBEL

The law of libel is too complex for this chapter to do more than flag the dangers that exist in almost every newspaper story. These are some basic observations. You will benefit from reading up the subject at length. You should learn to recognize what might get you into trouble in your own stories, for it is surprisingly easy to miss something. Some journalists think it is part of the game to get pieces into the paper without the lawyer noticing. You will do better to ensure that all contentious work is seen by lawyers. Sometimes a session with a newspaper lawyer not only covers the paper legally but also sharpens up your copy.

The classic definition of a libel is a statement about someone that lowers him in the estimation of right-thinking people generally or brings him into ridicule and contempt. What amounts to ridicule and contempt? Who are right-thinking people? Those are matters for the law to develop, which is why so much of what you write is capable of being libellous.

Let's get some misunderstood points out of the way. The fact that you are merely reporting the views of others is no defence. You are liable for all the statements in your story, whether they are made by you or by an interviewee. The quote marks offer no protection. If, on the other hand, what you say in the story is true and you can prove it to be so, you have a defence. But if someone takes you to court for libel, it is up to you to prove that what you wrote was true, not for him to prove that it wasn't.

It is clear that you are running the risk of libel when you accuse a businessman of running a fraudulent operation. It is less clear why it might be libellous to say of an actress that she is overweight, of a soap star that he is boring or of a quality Sunday newspaper editor that he is not fit to edit his paper because he spends his free time in nightclubs. But all three have fought libel actions. Matters of opinion can be dangerous when they concern the professional life of the people you are writing about. And remember that the qualities of the person you are writing about are relevant. While it might be libellous to accuse a dancer of being fat – obesity might lower such a performer in the eyes of right-thinking people – it would not be a problem to attach the same quality to a chef. To accuse a bachelor of sleeping with a woman is unlikely to be libellous. To accuse a Catholic priest of doing the same would be.

There are circumstances in which what you write is free from the risks of libel, however contentious. The clearest are when you are providing an accurate account of proceedings in a court case, or from the Houses of Parliament. Those proceedings are 'privileged', which is to say that you are entitled to report them, so long as you do so fairly and accurately.

There are signs that British law is keen to establish the principle of qualified privilege, where you do not have to prove that what you report is right, but you have to establish that you were justified, for public interest reasons, in printing it. This again is complex territory.

On the other hand, there are many circumstances in which the law should be your friend. Just as there are many things it appears to stop you doing, there are others that it insists you have the right to do. Many journalists have won important points of principle in their right to identify the subjects of court proceedings or to publish other material that is in the public domain.

Whatever you do, don't be cowed by the difficulties. Start by assuming that you can write what you like, then start editing on the basis of what the law will allow, remembering that the law is often not clear. If you do it the other way round – and write only what you know is entirely legally safe from the start – you start to run scared of lawyers. And that is something journalists must never do.

8

But what will you do when you are forty?

There may be more satisfying things than seeing your words in print for the first time, but there can't be many. If you really want to be a journalist, the chances are you started with your school magazine or student newspaper. Or you have been bombarding the letters page of your local paper.

This was how my big brother started. The *Star* in Sheffield had a Saturday evening football paper printed on green paper and called, reasonably enough, the *Green 'Un* (this was in the days before newspapers sought assistance from focus groups before deciding what title might impress readers). Each week the *Green 'Un* offered readers a few pounds for the best sports letter printed on the Tell It to Tony page, Tony being the first name of the chief football writer.

My brother was a student at the time, and supplemented his grant by writing under a series of pseudonyms. His proudest moment came when Sheffield Wednesday – then on one of their periodic descents of the Football League – were playing with a feckless red-haired winger, signed for very little from a Scottish club and much vilified by the home fans.

My brother wrote a short letter, purporting to be an Italian working as a waiter in Sheffield. It was, he wrote, a magical experience to watch football at Hillsborough. And in Archie Irvine, the clever winger with the fast feet, Wednesday had a gem that compared with any of the stars this waiter had seen playing for his home club, Inter Milan, at the San Siro stadium. Surely, suggested the waiter, it was only a matter of time before one of the big Italian clubs came in for him.

I often wondered if poor Archie Irvine cheered up on reading the letter, or whether he wondered why the Milanese scouts never showed up. But my brother made another £3, which in those days was enough to keep a student in drink for a weekend.

Actually, the letters page spoils you, for it guarantees not only your words but also a by-line. There you are, by name, often in bold print. And your words may be cut down, but they aren't changed much. When you start writing for newspapers, it may take time before your work is good enough to get your name above it. And even then you might not recognize the words below.

You can spend weeks as a trainee on a local newspaper, for example, before you actually get a story in the paper with your name attached to it. You may be quietly thrilled to see your words appear under pictures of elderly couples celebrating their golden wedding anniversaries. Then, a couple of days later, the paper comes out with four paragraphs about a burglary, printed almost as you wrote them. After that, joy oh joy, the tale about the West Highland terrier that swallowed the door key appears not only with pictures of the terrier, its X-rays and his owners, but also under your name. You are in business.

For the dedicated newsman or woman, there are peaks still to conquer, of course. Your first-page lead – that's the story at the top of the page; your first front-page story; your first splash – the story that leads the paper. On a day like that you probably want to buy drinks for all your colleagues, before going home to show the paper to your girlfriend. Or your boyfriend. Or your mum.

There are other landmarks: your first feature, your first colour piece – those are the ones where you are allowed to use adjectives other than 'massive', 'tragic' and 'horrific' – and your first permitted use of the pronouns 'I' and 'me' in copy, as in: 'I watched amazed as . . .' and 'The stunned dad of seven told me . . .'

Then there is the picture by-line – that's when you get not only your name but also your mugshot alongside it – typically awarded when you have been very brave, uncovered a terrific story or made yourself a figure of fun covering that sure-fire comic story the news desk handed out in the morning. You know the kind of thing: you are sent out to prove the truth of the survey that suggests most men don't know how to boil an egg; a local night school is giving lessons in romance; a nearby naturist club is holding an open day. Me, I got the chance to play darts with the British ladies' champion, a South Yorkshire pub landlady. The idea was that it would be humiliating for a man to be beaten by a woman. How Sheffield readers must have chuckled at that one.

If you are really doing well, you may become one of those reporters granted an automatic picture by-line, whether it is above a column – another sure sign of success – or news stories. The editor has decided that you are becoming a local celebrity whose mugshot pleases readers, or that you are about to go off to another job, and printing your picture in the paper will keep you happy.

These are the public milestones that you will pass on a local paper. Each one increases your confidence. Others are more private: the first time you successfully come back from interviewing a grieving mother with a picture of her dead child; the first story that you get from one of the contacts you have started to nurture; the first court case where you are trusted to handle running copy on your own, filing straight from your notebook with minutes to go to deadline.

But what happens when you feel you can do all those things? What do you do when you begin to feel you are no longer learning things? Is it time to move on?

That depends on what you really want from journalism. Many journalists move early in their careers – typically from a weekly to an evening paper – before putting down roots. We have discussed elsewhere why many journalists would not dream of leaving provincial papers, whether because of those roots or because they feel that journalism is a better, more honest trade at local level. For others, the provinces are merely the place to start, the place they can learn the business before making an assault on Fleet Street. If that is what you want to do, how do you make the leap?

The first thing you learn is that national papers, unlike the locals, rarely advertise for staff. The *Guardian* media page, *UK Press Gazette* and, more recently, holdthefrontpage.co.uk, a website run by four regional publishers, Northcliffe, Newsquest, Trinity Mirror and Johnston Press, all offer jobs around the provinces every week. There are other websites, such as www.journalism.co.uk, where you will find job ads. The regional publishers also put vacancies up on their own websites. If, to use the language of typical ads, you are a 'self-starter' or you are 'up for a challenge' or you 'want to set the news agenda', any number of provincial editors are looking for you.

But national editors tend to work to a different principle, which is that if you are good enough and ambitious enough, you will find them.

When I started, I believed that no national news editor would even consider talking to me until I had at least 120-words-a-minute shorthand, a proficiency certificate from the National Council for the Training of Journalists and a folder of front-page cuttings.

Years later, when I became a news editor myself and saw the job applications, I realized that everyone had folders of page one splashes to show me. As for the proficiency certificate and the shorthand, I am not sure I even asked. I gave them shifts and decided on the basis of a few stories whether they were any good.

That is how it worked when I started and that is how it works now. Don't think you are going to walk straight into a job. If you are lucky, you might get enough shifts to show what you can do.

The problem with shifts, of course, is that you need to be available to do them. If you work in or near London, you may be able to fit in some night work around your day job. On that basis, you have a clear advantage if your local paper is local to London, or near enough to get in and out easily. You may find other opportunities if you are working in the trade press, provided that your specialization is interesting enough to make something in newspapers looking for a general audience.

If you are in the provinces, the only way you are likely to get on to Fleet Street is to resign your job and take a chance. It is a nice gamble. The prize is regular work leading to a full-time job. The stake is security. Are you ready to leave your comfortable job and nice flat in the provinces for all the insecurity of shifting in London?

If you are, don't be daunted by the work itself. If you are half-way competent, the people who surround you in a national news-room will not run rings round you. On the contrary, you may be surprised how far a little hard work will take you. I said earlier that news editors might not worry about NCTJ certificates, but there is no doubt that having that qualification adds to your confidence. You are likely to be picking up night shifts where, usually, little happens. But if you are there on the night something does, you may be able to make your reputation.

That was the kind of fluke that led in my case to a job at the *Sunday Times*. This was before the age of mobile phones, when if you did not find people at home when you phoned, you did not find them at all. I happened to be at home one Saturday morning, shortly after a mad young man fired at the Queen with a starting pistol, as she rode to the Trooping the Colour ceremony. This was a big news story, and the *Sunday Times* news desk urgently needed casual reporters to supplement the staff reporters already at work.

It was nothing but luck that I was in when they called. It was further good fortune that they liked the cuts piece I knocked off after rushing to the office. At any rate, they liked it enough to ask me back for more shifts, which was when I learned that they had been looking for a young reporter with provincial experience. Several had been interviewed. All had been a little too cocky. Thank heavens I had made a habit of getting in the teas. Within a few weeks, a job was mine. What would have happened if I had arrived in London a month later?

The invitation from the *Sunday Times* also taught me another lesson that holds true on national papers twenty-five years later: they like you best when someone else is after you.

I had been doing regular shifts on the *Daily Mail* for some weeks before the *Sunday Times* job came up. The minute I explained that I would be unable to do any more because I had been offered a job elsewhere, the *Mail* suddenly decided I had a future with them too. Until then, there had been no guarantees of work.

Now the deputy news editor, who had barely acknowledged me during the previous two months, appeared at my desk and suggested we have a drink to discuss the future. Paul Dacre – who was to become, fifteen years later, a spectacular success as editor of the paper – tried to explain why a six-month contract with the *Mail* would be much better for me than a staff job at the *Sunday Times*. The contract was all ready, why didn't I just come back to the office with him and sign it now?

You decide: a contract with the *Mail* with no time off, no holiday pay and no guarantee of a future beyond six months, or a staff job at the *Sunday Times*. Yes, that's what I thought too.

What worked in my favour then will work in yours today. Journalism is a free market: you are in your most powerful bargaining position when others want you. Newspapers that have happily run your pieces on an ad hoc basis begin to offer you a better deal when they think you might take your work elsewhere. Occasional features turn into freelance contracts. Shifts become jobs. Junior jobs in the newsroom rise to specialist posts.

Similarly, once you are in, your best chance of a pay rise is to find someone who is prepared to pay you more. Many of my colleagues have built up their pay on the basis of better offers from rivals. What's more, they have never been asked actually to produce evidence of those offers.

Did the offers exist? That is a very good question. Who knows? But it is amazing how quickly word gets around that an ambitious reporter has been seen having a drink with the news editor of a rival paper – so quickly that you might even think that the ambitious reporter has been spreading the news himself.

But if you're thinking what I think you're thinking, be careful. If you've decided that, to secure an exciting new job or a fat pay rise, you have only to walk in to see the editor with a job offer from a rival in your pocket, you are mistaken.

How many times have I secretly clenched a fist in triumph when someone I have been dying to get rid of has walked in to announce he plans to go elsewhere? If I were honest and open, I would be expressing amazement that anyone else should want them but, being nicely brought up, I make the usual remarks about what a fantastic opportunity it is and how grateful I am for all the fine work they have done.

There are others who come in who, certainly, will be missed. But companies frequently go through budget periods when they decide that they will offer nothing more than flattery as a means of dissuading journalists from going elsewhere. The truth is that the industry depends on a movement of talent. If you don't juggle the staffs around, everyone becomes a little stale. Having people move out creates the opportunity to have new people move in. Only occasionally have I gone straight to management to try to secure enough money to persuade someone to stay.

This is why it is a dangerous game to play if you either have no offer, or you are not prepared to take it up. Imagine going in to see the editor confident that he will come up with an extra £5,000 and walking out having been told that he doesn't feel he should stand in your way of such an exciting new challenge? I have made it a rule never to seek more money on the basis of a job elsewhere unless I am committed in principle to moving.

I have seen too many journalists 'back out' of moves that, hours before, they were describing as wonderful challenges with lots of money. Suddenly, even though their existing editor has failed to come up with another pound in salary, the man or woman with the exciting job offer has decided to stay after all. It is enough to make you wonder whether the job offer existed.

Talks such as these are not just about pay. The alternative job offer is still the fastest way to create a move for yourself, even if it is within the paper for which you already work. Provided your paper really wants you, this is your chance to move to the role you have always coveted, your power to do so being dependent on your being more in favour than the person currently holding the job you want.

This is your opportunity to explain that you have always really wanted to report politics, or to work for the foreign desk, or to make the move into management as the editor of a section.

Do not go in to give notice without having thought what might keep you where you are. If you have made enough of an impression for them to want to keep you at all, now is your chance to say what you really want to do. For a few golden hours you can make yourself the centre of attention, with everyone wanting to be your friend. You might be able to make yourself even more golden by explaining what it is that would make you stay. However outrageous your demand may be, make it when you have the chance. The worst that can happen is that they will say no.

Remember, however, that this happy period does not last for ever. You will be allowed to indulge yourself for a while. They will be happy for you to have a day or two to think about things. But once you turn the decision into a real drama, once you start going back and forth, they will begin to lose interest. If you are not careful, you will turn that wonderful eagerness on their part into a sullen irritation.

The last thing you want to do is take so long to decide to stay, and make so many demands, that they begin to wish they had never bothered. Negotiations like these are a very fine balance, just like real-life romances. Employers who feel you are beginning to play them along begin to wonder what they saw in you. That initial inclination to persuade you to stay at all costs is replaced by a desire to have you out of the building as soon as possible.

And don't expect the love-in to continue once you decide you are on your way. Then they will want you out as soon as they can. Editors who were stopping you in the corridor to say how much they admired your latest piece are suddenly looking right through you. Psychologically, they are now thinking only of the journalist who is going to replace you. So don't be surprised when your friends describe the latest opinions of your talent.

'He's nothing like as good as he thinks he is.' 'She's been made to look good by the subs.' 'He'll soon find out how tough it is when he's expected to come up with his own stories.' 'What a pain! Who does she think she is? We are better off without her. We can hire better talent on half her money.'

I suggested you use those opportunities when people think well of you to push for what you really want to do. But what *do* you really want? Many journalists find it hard to decide.

In those first few years, nothing can ever seem as much fun as the life of a general reporter. It brings a remarkable mix of subjects and an uncertainty each day that can remain enthralling. Certainly it continues to enthral many who would not dream of doing anything else.

But is it, as they say, a life for grown-ups? Once you are a little older, don't you want greater control over your life than the whims and caprices of news? Wouldn't you rather specialize, and build up some real knowledge about a subject?

And what happens when you do age and suddenly all those stories that seemed so important when you were younger don't seem to matter so much? I have known more than one sports writer, at the peak of his profession, wake up one morning and ask if this is all there is. Their peers think they have the best jobs in the world: they worry that sport means nothing compared to the bigger issues of the day.

Certainly sports writing is what many reporters would wish to do, though for those eager to keep writing, the most popular jobs change. My generation grew up wanting to be investigative reporters or foreign 'firemen', the staff journalists who get sent abroad when wars, famine and disaster happen. The keenest among us were always going off to the British Airways health centre to keep up the inoculations needed for Third World hot spots. They would write off to minor embassies, seeking the visas needed for Godforsaken areas of the world, just in case a story broke there. Then, a few years later, there was a vogue for politics, and ambitious reporters were desperate to get down to Westminster. Now the hot spot is show business or column writing.

You will discover that there is no clear rationale to scales of pay. Rather, reporters and writers are paid whatever they have managed to negotiate at some point in their career. Some of the laziest people in the office may be pulling in big money on the basis of a barely remembered success in the past. The go-getters may not yet be getting the financial reward that their go-getting deserves. And just as show business rewards the 'talent', so section heads may earn less than many of the big name journalists that they employ.

If you decide instead to climb the newspaper hierarchy, be warned that there is no obvious way up. There are editors who have not written a story since moving to the subs' desk within months of being cub reporters. There are editors who have never run a section or issued an instruction to another journalist but who are summoned from glorious careers as writers to run an entire paper.

But, for every paper, there can be just one editor. Just as you think you are getting somewhere on the ladder, in comes someone from outside to step on the next rung. Deputy editors wait eagerly for their editor to fall under a bus, only to watch impotently as a new character impresses the proprietor and barges in ahead.

On the other hand, journalism is a forgiving business. If you can find a story, or write a piece, or sub copy, there will always be work for you. Some of the happiest journalists I have met have worked their way up a hierarchy, worked as managers or been an editor. But what they really like – really really like – is going back to where they were. To being writers, and seeing their stuff in print.

The *Daily Telegraph*'s Bill Deedes found the life so irresistible that he went back to it even after alternative existences as a Cabinet minister and an editor. In his ninety-first year he continued to travel the world as a reporter. Peter Preston, the celebrated editor of the *Guardian*, transformed himself happily into a columnist. Donald Trelford, editor of the *Observer*, realized how much he enjoyed writing about sport.

These journalists have all played influential roles in national political and social events. And here they are happy to be reporting again. They demonstrate the merit of basic principles: of having something to say and wanting to say it; of asking questions and demanding answers; of regarding each edition of the newspaper as exciting as all the editions that have gone before it; above all, of appreciating that the joy of journalism is in seeing their pieces in print.

That, perhaps, is the most encouraging thing of all about the newspaper business. There are more writers than you think it can possibly want. But there is always room for another good one.

My Big Break II

Mark Henderson, science correspondent, *The Times* – joined September 1996, as graduate trainee

'I started on *The Times* via the graduate trainee scheme, in which 500-plus young journalists compete for two or three places a year. My feeling has always been that I got the job on the back of a piece I wrote for the *Observer* while on work experience there. I was at Oxford University, and had heard about two rival groups of students racing each other to compile the unofficial Norrington Table of college results and sell it to a national newspaper. It made a great talking-point story that gave my cuttings portfolio a centrepiece.

'When I started at *The Times*, I was lucky enough to join just before the 1997 general election. As one of the most junior reporters, I was assigned to the election research desk, which put me in direct contact with lots of influential reporters and editors and gave me an early chance to impress. As I did well, once the election was over and I went to the home news desk I was known and trusted by the rest of the team. That made for good assignments from a very early stage.'

Jo Elvin, editor, *Glamour* magazine

'I had been doing work experience at a teenage magazine in Sydney (where I'm from), just going in a couple of days a week, doing vox pops and research for them. Unbeknown to me there was a coup brewing and when the features team tried to get the editor ousted, it backfired and they were all sent packing. As I had been a more than eager unpaid assistant for some months and I could string a sentence together, I was asked to help out in the crisis. A few weeks later, I was offered a full-time job, promptly quit my BA in Communications degree, and never looked back.'

Ruth Gledhill, religion correspondent, *The Times*

'After a personal crisis I left Leeds University early and went to work for West Yorkshire Passenger Transport Executive, selling bus tickets. My lifelong ambition of being a journalist seemed beyond reach. Then an issue of public transport policy emerged that I felt so strongly about, I wrote to the *Yorkshire Post* to state my view. Seeing my letter in print made me realize that writing for a living might not be such an unrealistic hope after all. This motivated me to apply – successfully – to the London College of Printing to study journalism. Almost everything that I did there for my coursework I tried to get published, anywhere, for nothing. The London Newspaper Group used most of the stories. This gave me a huge cuttings folder to take to interviews. When applying for jobs at the end of my two-year course, I began writing to every single provincial newspaper, weekly and daily, in *Willings Press Guide*. The *Birmingham Post* offered me indentures.'

9

Why small papers are the big thing

For years it was all so simple. There were broadsheet papers and there were tabloid papers. But that was before the autumn of 2003, when the British newspaper industry suddenly changed direction.

The broadsheets were the so-called quality titles – the *Daily Telegraph*, *The Times*, the *Guardian*, the *Independent* and, at the end of the week, their Sunday siblings. They were often accused of 'dumbing down', but they were the kind of newspaper you could take home to meet your mother.

There is a research technique that market researchers play with focus groups. They ask: if this product were a person, what kind of person would it be? On that basis, quality newspapers would hold respectable jobs in the professions, teaching, and, in the case of the *Guardian*, the social services.

The tabloids, the *Sun*, the *Mirror* and the *Star* and, a little higher up the social scale, the *Mail* and the *Express*, were different. The tabloids were not so well brought up. If they were people, they would be fairground workers and ticket touts, nightclub acts and travelling salesmen: fun to spend time with, of course, but not necessarily reliable.

You only have to look at the papers themselves to see the distinction between the two groups of tabloid titles. The *Sun*, *Mirror* and *Star* are 'pops' – the 'popular press' – or 'red tops', after the colour of their mastheads. The *Mail* and the *Express* are 'middle market'.

But if you don't look at papers closely, it is easy to lump the tabloids together, which is what the British public tended to do. The term 'tabloid' took on a derogatory connotation. It became a synonym for 'intrusive', 'disreputable', 'unpleasant', 'prurient' and any other nasty adjectives you cared to think of.

In the words of the *Chambers Dictionary*: '**tabloid** (n) a newspaper of small-format, measuring *approx* 30×40cm (about 12×16in), *usu* rather informal or sensationalistic in style and with many photographs.'

The key word is sensationalistic. There was journalism, which was said to be a democratic good even by those politicians who didn't believe it to be so, and there were 'the tabloids'. The fact that someone had 'sold his story to a tabloid newspaper' was enough to convey that the vendor was not a proper person and that the story was unreliable. Britain was said to be embracing a 'tabloid culture'; the Labour government pandered to 'tabloid justice' in introducing new laws in areas of populist concern; stories ministers did not like were invariably condemned as 'tabloid frenzy'.

As you can imagine, it was galling for the *Mail* and the *Express* to find themselves lumped in with the other three tabloids. Why, until the 1970s, they had been broadsheets, even if they hadn't been able to claim the quality title too. There were very clear social nuances. I remember as a child hearing the kind of conversation at which middle-class Britain excelled. I was staying with my grandmother, in the rural North, as she replied to a friend who had asked if she took a quality newspaper, 'Oh yes, we get the *Sunday Express* every week.'

The *Sunday Express* was then a broadsheet, but my grandmother had left herself dangerously exposed. 'Oh no,' said her friend. 'That is a popular paper, not a quality paper.'

I doubt such distinctions bothered Richard Desmond, who bought the *Express* after making money out of soft-core pornography, but journalists at the *Mail* have always been eager to position the paper differently.

The late Sir David English, who transformed the paper to tabloid format, tried when he did so to get a new term into popular usage. The *Mail* was not a tabloid, he explained. It was a 'qualoid', for 'quality tabloid'. Sadly, the term never took off, though the *Mail* did. The man who followed him as editor, Paul Dacre, was also at pains to proclaim that his paper was a quality newspaper and pointed to his stable of former broadsheet writers to justify the claim. Some journalists moved easily from broadsheet to tabloid markets, yet it seemed that the distinctions were set in stone.

Broadsheet journalists referred patronizingly to stories in 'down-market tabloids'. Tabloid journalists, comforting themselves with the fact that their journalism sold well even if it did not achieve critical acclaim, retaliated with references to the 'unpopular press'. Nothing irritated tabloid journalists more than seeing broadsheet papers run tabloid-style stories under the pretext that they were reporting what the tabloids were saying, rather than chasing the same interests.

Yet it was becoming clear that these rules about size made little sense to a new generation. A younger audience was mystified about the point of a broadsheet: how and where could you read it? Why couldn't it be neater to hold? How could you read it on crowded buses and trains? What was the point of a newspaper that you had to spread out on the floor? This new generation was already getting news from alternative sources. If papers were hard to handle, would younger people stop reading them altogether?

The logic was to go small, but the fear was that tabloid papers in Britain were so closely associated with the popular end of the market that no reader would be prepared to accept tabloid size from a quality paper.

Strangely, the size of papers had never been a problem out of Britain. American papers tended to be a size that, if not quite tabloid, was smaller than broadsheet. In Europe it was simply not an issue: most of the papers were small, including properly intelligent ones such as *Le Monde*.

Could you get away with it in Britain? The *Independent* decided to give it a go. But rather than change overnight into a tabloid, the paper resolved to offer readers a choice. They could have the same paper in broadsheet or tabloid form.

The next problem was design. If you tell journalists to come up with a tabloid, their natural inclination is to give you something that looks like the *Daily Mail*. But once you start doing that, you inevitably start taking different editorial decisions. There would be, for example, a natural inclination to go for the kind of emotional splashes in which tabloid papers specialized: splashes that had real impact.

But if you printed a broadsheet version of the paper with one splash and a tabloid version with another splash, which would be the real paper? Would the tabloid paper throw out stories that ran too long, even though they were printed in full in the broadsheet? Would it concentrate on big picture spreads, like other tabloids?

What's more, no one can do the *Mail* as well as the *Mail* can do it: it was clear that trying to ape existing tabloids would take any quality paper into a battle it could not hope to win.

In the summer of 2003 several broadsheets began to experiment with creating tabloids that reproduced the look and feel of their broadsheet parents in tabloid form. The idea was not to look like a bad copy of the *Mail*, but like a reduced version of the broadsheet.

The task was to come up with a tabloid version of the paper so close to the broadsheet that, if one reader read the tabloid version and the other the broadsheet, they would feel, to use the language of the marketing department, that they had had the same 'reading experience'.

This solution, which seems to have occurred to all the broadsheets at about the same time, was a breakthrough in design and in editorial philosophy: once you took this route there was no longer any concern that the broadsheet and tabloid versions of the paper would offer differing news and views. They would be the same paper, only in different format. Just as Coca Cola is Coke whether it comes out of a tin or a bottle, so newspapers could offer the same quality journalism in broadsheet and tabloid.

To all journalists, this alternative version of the paper was a tabloid. But, mindful of the unattractive baggage that the word carried for many broadsheet readers, the *Independent* felt it would be less of a risk if they came up with an alternative word to describe the reduced size. That is where the term 'compact' came in.

The *Independent* launched its new version of the paper with a poster, radio and television advertising campaign that stressed the beauty of having a choice. Whether it was big or small, it was still the *Independent*. The newspaper industry held its breath – and discovered that readers liked the smaller size.

The roll-out of the tabloid started in London, where there seemed to be a ready market among commuters. Here was a paper that you could read on the bus or the Tube. Pretty soon the paper made the tabloid available in more regions, and, eventually, nationally. As managers pored over the figures, one thing became clear. The tabloid version was attracting existing readers of the paper – it had always expected a degree of cannibalization – and new readers. But the new readers did not seem to be coming from other titles. It seemed that the tabloid was either bringing in readers who had previously bought the paper only occasionally or readers who had not previously bought a paper at all.

Within weeks the *Independent* compact had put paid to the notion that British readers would never accept a quality newspaper in tabloid form. And, as the paper became available throughout the country, it was clearly not only commuters who took to the new look.

Within six months, the paper saw its circulation rise by almost a quarter. Admittedly, that was from a low base of around 200,000, just over half what the *Guardian* sold and less than a quarter of the sale of the *Daily Telegraph*. But after years of decline, it was a boost not only to sales but also to morale at the paper.

Less than a couple of months after the *Independent*'s lead, *The Times* followed, producing a tabloid version that also looked much like the broadsheet parent. That too began to take off, adding about 40,000 sales to the paper as the tabloid version was made available across the country.

Journalists on the popular tabloids were unimpressed. These new versions were not proper tabloids, they said. Where were the design tricks? Where was the clever use of pictures? Where was the lightness of touch? If these papers had really wanted to be innovative, they argued, they should have developed radical new designs.

Not all broadsheet editors thought it was a good idea, either. As the *Guardian* editor Alan Rusbridger pointed out, the natural tendency to put just one story on the front page was fine when there was a big story around, but looked too loud when there wasn't. If you got into the habit of running with just one story on the front, what did you do when you really wanted to make an impact?

The *Daily Telegraph* hung back, unconvinced that the tabloid made economic sense. As far as editorial was concerned, it was an obvious benefit. Journalists like selling more papers. Clearly the tabloid was a means of doing that. But the commercial departments of the paper were not so sure. Advertisers had always paid more for broadsheet papers than for tabloids, and made it clear that they were not particularly excited at the idea of a paper splitting its readership between broadsheet and tabloid formats, even if the overall number of sales was higher.

Furthermore, whatever you gained in circulation had to be compared with the cost of producing two papers at once. Everyone agreed that, once you started, there could be no going back. Readers who had warmed to a tabloid would not thank you for withdrawing it from sale.

Yet what would happen if you went tabloid completely? How many readers would stop buying you because they preferred the broadsheet? The logic was that you would have to produce both versions for years, with all the costs.

There was a vigorous debate at the *Independent*, where some in management argued for going completely tabloid and others pointed out that, as the paper had just run an expensive advertising campaign that promised readers the choice, it would be unwise to take that choice away.

The paper decided to experiment further, and announced that its

Saturday edition would be available only in tabloid form. Saturday is not a commuting day, so this scheme would demonstrate further whether readers really wanted a tabloid for itself, rather than as an easier paper to read on a commute. They did. The *Independent*'s Saturday sale, which had been falling fast, began to climb.

Over at *The Times*, the tabloid experiment was less convincing. The paper attempted to encourage readers to take the smaller version, but encountered opposition. Readers seemed to like the tabloid when the choice to buy it was their own, but to resent having it delivered instead of the broadsheet.

The *Independent* had successfully turned the balance to the point where more readers wanted the tabloid than wanted the broadsheet. That meant they could give priority to the production of the tabloid, which meant, in turn, that designers could improve and polish the compact look.

For *The Times*, that wasn't an option. Readers wanted the broadsheet more. At best, the paper found a 50–50 split. To cope with that kind of demand, the broadsheet had to come first. The tabloid was put together each night at great speed, by a team inheriting the work already done on the broadsheet. *The Times* had never promised readers that everything in the broadsheet would also be in the tabloid, but there had been an implicit promise to that effect. As the weeks wore on, it became clear that there were substantial gaps between what appeared in the two papers bearing the *Times* masthead each day.

As for the *Guardian*, it fell into a terrible depression. For years it had prided itself on its design flair and reputation for innovation. Now the *Independent*, the paper that it believed it had fought and beaten, had stolen its clothes. Suddenly everyone was talking about the *Independent*'s coup. Everyone wanted to interview its editor, Simon Kelner. The only thing they wanted to know about the *Guardian* was whether it would follow its rival's lead.

That excitement came to a head at the British Press Awards in March 2004, when *The Independent* was named Newspaper of the Year by a group of former newspaper editors. This is always a controversial prize. Should it go to a paper that is consistently good, week after week? Or to a paper that is seen to have done something different in the previous year? If it is to the first, then many journalists in national papers would set aside doubts about its political line and vote for the *Daily Mail*. It is an extraordinarily professional newspaper, edition after edition after edition. Perhaps that is why the editor of the *Mail* turned up to the awards ceremony with his senior staff: the last-minute word was that his paper was to win the top award yet again. But as often as not, the prize goes to the paper that has done something different. As Simon Kelner took the stage to receive the award and to attack those who had said his paper was on its last legs, the *Mail* team hardly troubled to disguise its irritation. No one would have argued that the *Independent* had been consistently better than its rivals. But it had changed the face of journalism. Now it decided it was safe to move entirely to tabloid production.

The award must have troubled further the sleep of the *Guardian* editor, Alan Rusbridger. He had already drawn up tabloid dummies that were admired by focus groups of readers. But he had decided early on that, come what may, the *Guardian* would not run two versions. It would go completely tabloid, stay broadsheet or find something entirely different. Early in 2004, Mr Rusbridger put a waiting world out of its misery. The *Guardian*, he announced, would not be going tabloid. That did not mean, he emphasized, that it would necessarily stay broadsheet.

Mr Rusbridger had in mind the 'something different'. He wanted the continental look, half-way between a tabloid and a broadsheet. Designing it was no problem. But how was he going to print it? The *Guardian*'s printing presses could handle a tabloid or a broadsheet. To produce something in between would mean finding new presses or cutting off several inches of surplus paper each night. It was certainly possible to make that cut, but it would cost time and – in wasted paper – several millions of pounds more a year. And how would environmentally conscious *Guardian* readers react to the news that their favourite paper was now wasting several forests purely to achieve a new look?

The early plans were revised and, in 2004, the *Guardian* announced a £50 million investment in printing presses that would allow it to produce a newspaper based on European designs – something between the British tabloid and the British broadsheet. This would give the *Guardian* the new look it craved, but was there a danger that, in buying presses to deliver that new design, it was limiting its future options?

Those options were still under review at the *Daily Telegraph*, which, perhaps more by luck than judgement, had avoided the problems that beset *The Times*. There, attempts to push all readers towards the tabloid were still failing. While the paper had picked up as many as 30,000 extra sales, it was a costly operation to produce two versions of the same paper each night. It was also difficult to pacify those traditionally-minded readers who reacted angrily when they found there were only tabloid versions of their paper left on sale.

Could there be mileage for the *Telegraph* in remaining the only broadsheet newspaper? Would it be possible to lure some of those disaffected *Times* readers? On the other hand, if the tabloid newspaper were the future, was there a danger that the *Telegraph* would become part of history? To make things more complicated still, the Telegraph Group was up for sale: until the new ownership was sorted out, there was no chance of taking the decision to change the format.

What was not in doubt was that there had been a revolution. The *Independent* cheerfully suggested that the *Oxford English Dictionary* take up a new definition of 'broadsheet': '1 (n) newspaper in a large format. 2 (adj) tired, staid, out-of-date, lacking in ideas.'

It based its cheeky assumption on a quote in *NME* from an American musician, commenting on the band Wilco: 'I think Wilco are unfairly tainted as being some kind of broadsheet, elderly, rock-magazine darlings, and I have always thought that they are so much more exciting and innovative.'

If the next generations think only the compact, tabloid newspaper can be exciting and innovative, then the days of the broadsheet are surely over.

10

Is journalism moral?

'Every journalist who is not too stupid or too full of himself to notice knows what he does is indefensible.' That is how the *New Yorker* writer Janet Malcolm sees the business of reporting, at the start of her book *The Journalist and the Murderer*, a documentary account of the relationship between a convicted murderer and the journalist whom he believed to be his friend.

Heavens, that's quite an indictment – and there we were setting ourselves up as good, brave defenders of democracy. Didn't we promise to expose wrongdoers, protect the weak, and shine torches of truth into dark corners? Are we deluding ourselves? Is the reality that we are merely seeking interesting travel, varied work and a picture by-line?

If we accept the view of Ms Malcolm, the contact between journalist and those to whom he talks is to the advantage of only one party. And it is not the interviewee. Is successful journalism necessarily to the detriment of those we write about? Far from being indefensible, shouldn't this business be capable of being defended by all who believe in democracy?

In a typically readable introduction to a new edition of Janet Malcolm's book, published by Granta, the journalist Ian Jack suggests that Ms Malcolm had in mind only the particular form of journalism that is the subject of her book – the kind that is dependent on the relationship between journalist and subject.

The journalist draws his – or her – subject out, probably by pretending to a sympathy that he does not feel. The technique is dissected coldly by Ms Malcolm: 'He is a kind of confidence man, preying on people's vanity, ignorance or loneliness.'

You can see how the description applies to the relationship she writes about, where the convicted murderer believes that the journalist with whom he collaborates on a book is convinced of his innocence. Only when the work is published does it become clear that, far from believing in the prisoner's innocence, the journalist has been sure of his guilt almost from the start. He has used sympathy as a means of getting close to his subject.

Ms Malcolm's words would certainly be easier to swallow if – as Mr Jack suggests – they were to be applied only to the kind of journalism she was writing about. That way we can leave the local reporter who writes up a golden wedding to work with a clear conscience.

Inevitably, when we take her accusation to extremes such as the weekly report of wedding anniversaries, we quickly make it look absurd. I have yet to meet the reporter who can turn the wisdom of those years of marriage – 'Never let the sun go down on a quarrel' – into a reflection of his own ego. There are many areas of journalism that can be held up as a clear public good. Are war reporting, investigations into council corruption and revelations of business wrongdoing worthless activities? Are those thousands of words in the papers every day really of benefit only to the journalists who write them?

Yet it is hard to work in journalism without acknowledging that there is something in what Ms Malcolm writes. Fortunately, the interests of democracy and journalism often coincide. We *are* out there with our torches. But, whatever they might claim, journalists tend not to be driven by the sense of public service you expect to find in police, fire fighters and soldiers.

Unlike members of those other groups, journalists have to turn their activities into something interesting enough to sell newspapers. A story, in the end, works only if people want to read it. Newspapers and magazines are published to make money. Public servants may go about their work in a selfless fashion, journalists don't. They are egocentric. They like by-lines. They are in show business. Some of them just don't admit it.

How, for instance, do Ms Malcolm's words play following the suicide of David Kelly? On the basis of his interview with Dr Kelly, the BBC *Today* programme reporter Andrew Gilligan reported that Downing Street had knowingly exaggerated the threat posed by weapons of mass destruction held by the Iraqi leader, Saddam Hussein. The government rejected the claim with some vehemence. The BBC stood by the report, the then Chairman, Gavyn Davies, and the then Director General, Greg Dyke, rejecting criticism of it from the man who was Tony Blair's chief press adviser at the time, Alastair Campbell. It emerged that Mr Gilligan's source was Dr Kelly, who was called before a parliamentary inquiry. A little later, his body was discovered in countryside near his home.

A public inquiry was led by Lord Hutton, a senior judge, who cleared the government of leaking Dr Kelly's name to the press and was highly critical of the standards of reporting by the BBC in the case. His report led to the resignation from the BBC of Mr Davies, Mr Dyke and Mr Gilligan.

The report did nothing to end controversy about the war, with many continuing to question the circumstances in which the government went to war and to back the BBC, despite the law lord's criticisms. It also raised debate about journalistic standards and what should be expected of the BBC. Some said Mr Gilligan had engaged in inaccurate reporting of an amateurish kind, that he had pushed a story too far and jeopardized the entire reputation of the BBC. There were colleagues who came forward to say they had always known he was a loose cannon. But many others backed him on the basis that his story, while flawed in some detail, was broadly correct. This, they argued, was good and important journalism, scrutinizing government actions. The *Spectator* magazine, edited by the Conservative MP Boris Johnson, made Mr Gilligan its defence and diplomatic editor.

As the arguments continued, it became a given that the standards to be expected of the BBC were higher than those of Sunday newspapers. The Sunday titles had long had a reputation for inflating stories on the back of limited facts in order to make news each weekend. The *Sunday Times*, in particular, was frequently accused by journalists on other broadsheets of running stories whose headlines and intros promised more than the detail below delivered.

According to that view, Andrew Gilligan's report would have been fine for a Sunday paper. But the BBC had a responsibility to report objective news rather than rush to broadcast scoops that had not been rigorously researched.

As a former Sunday newspaper journalist, I identified readily with the Gilligan story. Indeed, he had worked for me successfully in my years at the *Sunday Telegraph*, where he had been punctilious in seeking to separate fact from supposition. Had he become more slack in his ways? Were my standards as a Sunday journalist too low? Could you get away with things on a privately funded newspaper that you could not get away with as a broadcaster funded by the licence payer?

Certainly, while the piece was right in essence – there were members of the intelligence services who believed that the government had exaggerated the threat of Iraqi weapons of mass destruction – it was wrong in certain details, at least in an early morning report on the *Today* programme on Radio 4. At 6.07 am, in a 'two-way' interview with the presenter John Humphrys, Mr Gilligan suggested not only that the government had 'sexed up' an intelligence dossier on Saddam Hussein's weapons capability before the war but also that government officials were aware that the weapons claim was wrong when they did so.

There was enough here to raise all kinds of questions about ethical standards of journalism. How far can you rely on one source of information? Is an anonymous source to be given the same weight as the public announcements of the Prime Minister's office? Is it right to refer to a scientist from the Ministry of Defence as 'intelligence sources'? Should you run such pieces without calling government offices to give them a chance to make an official response? Given the duty of journalists to protect confidential sources, why did Mr Gilligan call members of a parliamentary committee and tell them they would benefit from asking certain questions of Dr Kelly when the Ministry of Defence scientist appeared before them?

Or did the ends justify the means? Was this such an important story that we should not be deflected by imperfections in the gathering of it? The world of journalism was left divided neatly down the middle, with as many ready to vilify Mr Gilligan as to laud him.

Let us look at the nature of Andrew Gilligan's contacts with David Kelly in the light of the criticism of journalism made by Janet Malcolm, quoted at the start of this chapter. She suggested, in essence, that the relationship between reporter and interviewee is what psychiatrists call an abusive one.

Did David Kelly know what he was getting into? Did Mr Gilligan betray his trust? If Mr Gilligan had obtained what appeared to be an important story from Dr Kelly, was that the end of his responsibility? Or did he owe some greater duty of care to the scientist?

Given his suicide, we will never know what Dr Kelly hoped to achieve by meeting Mr Gilligan. The pair had talked before. As a civil servant, Dr Kelly was not meant to have close, informal links with reporters. But it was clear that he had, for it transpired that he had helped a number of journalists who had asked for unattributable information.

Was it, to use Ms Malcolm's word, 'indefensible' that they had interviewed him, relying on him for information for their stories? If they were getting something out of it, so perhaps was he. There are many reasons why people help journalists and not all of them are entirely selfless.

We have only Mr Gilligan's account of his meeting with Dr Kelly, but from the testimony of those other journalists who had talked to the Ministry of Defence scientist, it appears that he was happy to answer questions about what was going on in Iraq. There remains some doubt about what he did tell Mr Gilligan, but there is no reason to doubt that he expected Mr Gilligan to make use of the material.

But did Dr Kelly recognize himself as the source – the single source – of Mr Gilligan's *Today* report? We cannot know. Judging from what he told his family, he did not. He also told a committee of MPs that he did not. Was that because Mr Gilligan had taken things too far, or because Dr Kelly was embarrassed that he had been revealed as the source?

The Kelly case reveals the uncertainties that lie at the heart of journalistic relationships. The interests of the journalist and the people to whom he talks may coincide but they are not necessarily the same. The journalist is constantly looking for a story. If it is in his interests to explain precisely what that story is – even on occasion to read it back to his interviewee – he will do so. On many occasions he will merely take the information to use as a piece of the jigsaw he is constructing.

That is one of the reasons why people are so rarely entirely happy with any newspaper piece to which they have contributed quotes. They imagined that the journalist was going to print everything they said, not only those bits that made them look silly, or angry, or sad. Why does the other person in the story get quoted at such length? How could the journalist miss the point?

But the journalist's point of view is not necessarily the same as theirs. He or she is assembling a mass of information of which the interviewee's comments form only a part. The journalist has other views, historical information or observations to add to the mix.

What is important, as he assembles this material, is to develop enough of a relationship to gather the information that he needs at the time. That may take a twenty-minute phone conversation for copy that amounts, in the finished article, to a couple of sentences. He will invest the necessary effort to get the material he needs.

Does this make him, as Ms Malcolm put it, a 'confidence man, preying on people's vanity, ignorance or loneliness'? Well, that's harsh – and, having worked with Andrew Gilligan and been highly impressed, it is not an accusation that I would throw at him – but it is true that journalists use a variety of means to get people to open up. Some of these may be the techniques of the conman, but I would be happier to call them the skills of the travelling salesman. In any case, shouldn't we look at the ends rather than the means?

Nor do these little tricks always work. I remember a young colleague on the *Star*, Sheffield, returning in a fury from a story where the gormless photographer he was working with had ruined his spiel. He was interviewing a young mother, whose child had been hurt in an accident.

'It's a terrible moment when you hear,' he said, not letting his own bachelor, childless state get in the way of empathy. 'I know if it was my kids, I'd be in a right state.'

'Blimey, Phil,' said the photographer, putting down his camera. 'I didn't know you were married.'

Some journalists become chameleons, adjusting their accents to those of the people to whom they are talking. Others keep their distance, hoping that a certain authority in their tone will make the interviewee feel obliged to talk. Are these techniques wicked? Surely not.

When I was a cub reporter in 1978, I was shown a film produced by the National Council for the Training of Journalists, designed to teach young reporters how to conduct an interview.

Judging by the black and white footage and the narrow lapels on the dark suits – did I imagine that they were all smoking as well? – it had been made in the early 1960s, around the time that British cinema was enjoying a renaissance with gritty kitchen-sink drama set among the working classes.

The voiceover explained that the young reporter in the film was ringing a trade union official for information about a strike. 'Our reporter has never met the official but in order to strike up a rapport, he is going to pretend that they are old friends.'

Cut to the young reporter, dialling the number. Cut to trade union official, picking up the phone. Cut to reporter: 'Hello, mate, Keith Sproggett from the *Mail*. Long time no speak. How's it going, mate?'

Cut to trade union official: 'Oh, hello. Nice to hear you again. What can I do for you?'

If only it were so easy. Yet the sad thing is, when anyone rings me in my office and puts on a cheery voice, I fall for it, assuming that we've met and that it would be rude to ask who they are. The young reporters who ring these days must have seen the same film. It is impossible to avoid a smile as they start off: 'Hello, mate. How are you keeping?'

The reporters who ring me say they are journalists and make it clear what they are writing about. I know the game, so I weigh every word in my reply and work out how it could look in print.

But there are plenty of people who speak to reporters who don't make it clear why they are ringing. It is a common technique to phone to discuss one thing while intending to write about another. There are plenty of people who are interviewed by reporters and are mildly surprised by one or two questions in the course of a long and innocent conversation. Then they open a paper to find that it is only the one or two questions that were actually of interest to the journalist.

They can't say that they have been misquoted, because the words are theirs. They look silly if they complain that they did not know the story was actually about the issue raised at the end. Yet they are left with a clear impression of having been conned.

Is this bad behaviour by the journalist? Is it indefensible? That depends on how far he or she has gone in creating a false impression and whether the story justifies it.

How do you behave? How far do you go? That is up to you. There are any number of approaches and techniques that you might use that will not fall foul of the Press Complaints Commission. But they will leave a bad impression with the people to whom you speak.

The danger is that you become so sure of the importance of what you do, of the value of your story or your newspaper, that you lose a sense of perspective. You've got your story – does it matter that the people to whom you have spoken are left bewildered, angry or embarrassed? Would it have been so hard to tell them the context in which you intended to place their comments? Have they done something wrong to deserve having you make fun of them in the way you describe them?

This kind of behaviour is easier to get away with on national newspapers than local ones. On local papers there is a chance that the people you have just let down will come round to the offices to find you. Do you want to be called down to reception to meet the woman you trashed in the paper last week? On national papers it is less likely.

But even if you are not motivated by a sense of treating others as you would have them treat you, common sense tells you it may not be a good idea to treat people unkindly. What happens the next time you want to speak to them? Many journalists are happy to humiliate those whom they think they will never need to speak to again. If they feel someone is going to be of use in the future, they approach matters differently.

This is not to say that you should not develop practical skills and techniques in talking to people. On the contrary, they are vital, though I still haven't decided whether the residents of a tough housing estate react better to the man with the central casting public-school accent who makes no attempt to change it or to the reporter whose voice – like that of Tony Blair – goes up and down the social scale depending on the audience. But you will ultimately be happier – or at least you will feel a more moral person – if you are generally straight with people who are straight with you.

When are you justified in using a little trickery? How far can you go in hiding your true purpose when you are talking to people as a reporter? It is impossible to say, but once you start, you shouldn't be surprised when people begin to wonder whether they can trust the press. To you your trickery is justified because it has got you the story: to them it was merely a piece of deceitful behaviour.

For some reason, a particular conversation sticks in my mind from a council flat on a tough estate in Sheffield, more than twenty-five years ago. There had been a murder at the bus station, the police had charged a young man and I had been sent round to see his mother.

It was never going to be a big story. The killing had all the hallmarks of 'gay bashing'. The murder suspect may well have allowed the man to pick him up on the promise of sex and then bludgeoned him to death and robbed him. All we wanted was a picture of the suspect, to illustrate the story when the case came to trial some months later.

Now, if you knock on the door belonging to the parents of a murder suspect and tell them you would like a picture of their son to put in the paper, they are unlikely to invite you in and hand it over. So you knock on the door and say you would like to talk about the terrible news about their boy and you manage to get inside by giving the general impression that you share their view that it must all be some terrible mistake.

Then, after they have kindly made you a cup of tea and you have agreed that it will all be sorted out soon and you have implied that you will try to get some information out of the police that might help them find out what is going on, you ask what he is like. Could it be mistaken identity perhaps? Do they happen to have a picture?

Of course they do, and you hold it and suggest that if they wouldn't mind lending it to you, it would be useful. You don't say why it would be useful, though you mutter something about publicizing the case in the hope that witnesses will come forward to say that it wasn't their boy. Then you get out of the flat, clutching the print, and get back sharpish to the office and hand it over to the picture desk to copy and return.

Now, this was not a wicked transaction. The paper might well have been able to pick up a picture of the young man from police at the end of the trial. No one's words are being twisted. The paper is telling no lies. If the young man is going to go around killing people, the family are bound to get upset one way or another even without the intervention of the local paper. It is, above all, a proper function of newspapers to report what is going on. The people of Sheffield have a right to look at the faces of young murderers. If the end is good, why worry about the means?

Yet there was an element of false pretences from the start of our conversation that still nags, perhaps because it was the first time I was conscious of practising to deceive, though there have been many since. They knew I was from a newspaper, but I wanted them to believe that I was more akin to a social worker than a young reporter merely anxious for a picture. By putting on my fictitious, sympathetic act, I ensured I would get a photograph from a worried mother who was not bright enough to realize what was going on.

Most journalists would not see any moral dilemma there. It is what reporters do on almost every doorstep. At a conference of the Society of Editors, I told the anecdote as an example of the daily behaviour of journalists that helped to explain why we were not universally trusted.

At the end of my talk, someone raised his hand: 'What on earth was wrong with the way you picked up a picture of a murder suspect?'

Journalistically, nothing. Looked at from our perspective, this was merely good reporting to secure a snap of a violent young man who had broken the law. And if you don't think you could work like that, then perhaps you should think again about becoming a reporter. Looked at from the perspective of a worried Sheffield family, however, this was a con trick by a nice young man who had knocked on the door suggesting he might be able to do something to help their son.

To that extent the episode justified the dismissive words of Janet Malcolm, the author whose quote starts this chapter: 'He is a kind of confidence man, preying on people's vanity, ignorance or loneliness.'

Let Ms Malcolm call them the tricks of confidence men, but they are in truth little different from the techniques used by any people whose work puts them in regular contact with members of the public.

Think of the way good salesmen and women behave in making customers buy things they didn't even know they wanted, remember the manner in which a waiter or waitress creates the right atmosphere for the diners to order the dishes the restaurant wants to sell; consider the approach of experienced police officers in encouraging their interviewees to tell them the things they want to know.

Some journalists pride themselves on their ability to handle 'human interest'. They can get a grieving mother to talk about her dead child, a celebrity to reveal the secrets of her marriage, a famous entertainer to explain that he is gay. Some work on the basis that they will never need to speak to the person concerned again. The one-off session is easier, and once the piece is printed, it is too late for the interviewee to do anything more than feel aggrieved. The best do it so well – and with such honesty – that they can go back again and again.

You will have to decide the uses to which you put these professional techniques and whether you are using them further than is justified by the public interest. Most people would agree that they are properly used in the exposure of wrongdoing. You may also find that some of those who complain the loudest that they have been mistreated often have the most to hide.

It is no good company directors complaining that journalists have arrived purporting to want a complimentary story about their business if what they have told the journalists allows them to write a critical one.

As a news editor, I quickly learned to distinguish complaints about quotes in stories. People with a strong case tended to explain that they had never said the words that appeared in quotes. That was worrying, though it was surprising how often a tape recording proved them wrong. Less worrying were the people who complained that their quotes had been taken out of context. The out-of-context argument was usually the defence of the man who knew he had said too much, but didn't want to admit it.

The examples given above have concentrated on news gathering, on those relatively short encounters devoted to obtaining a piece of information, a photograph, perhaps an introduction to someone else who can help.

But what about those longer encounters, the kind of continuing involvement of journalist and subject that was the subject of the Malcolm book? In the world of celebrity interviews there is now such suspicion on both sides that few stars want to give journalists the access that they used to.

The stars and their publicists are suspicious because they think the journalist is either interested in only one angle or is going to turn any unguarded comment into the main focus of the piece. The journalist is suspicious because he or she knows that the star will be heavily protected by publicists who will allow only the most anodyne comments.

Having worked with many of the journalists who specialize in these kinds of encounter, you do start to see why the stars prefer to let their work speak for itself. Do you want your appearance, your work, your opinions factored entirely through the medium of the journalist who comes to see you? Do you want to pick up a magazine three months after meeting this nice, sympathetic, almost sycophantic figure to find that your entire world has been trashed?

Do you want to be the vehicle by which he or she achieves a reputation for incisive interviewing through writing vicious pieces that dissect taste in clothes, seize on misplaced references or make you seem quite mad? You may leave the interview thinking it has gone very well and that the journalist who came to see you was sympathetic and sweet. If only you knew what he or she was carrying back to the office in notebook, tape recorder and head.

I blush still to think of the occasions when I have been that sympathetic journalist, noting even as I nodded kindly at the actress I was interviewing, those words that would damn her from her own mouth. It didn't seem wrong at the time. How thrilled I remember being to escape from big houses along the Thames, tape recorder safely stowed away. The interviews had passed so pleasantly that I would be sent off with a kiss. How were they to know the treachery that I planned in my heart?

You can imagine how easy it is to praise amateur poetry in a conversation – and how bad that poetry looks in print. Or how a woman who is kind enough to reveal her thoughts on reincarnation may be upset when those notions are splashed across a Sunday supplement. Even as you are egging them on to spill the lot, you can't help feeling you should advise them to clam up.

Looking back, it was not a proper way to earn a living. We should not be surprised that so many interviewees now prefer to meet in neutral territory – a restaurant or a hotel room perhaps – rather than have their personal tastes dissected and broadcast to a wider public by an essentially unsympathetic eye. That they are prepared to play at all shows how much they need the publicity.

Those with something to sell do at least gain from these transactions. Just as you adopt a friendly manner because you think it will lead to the best quotes, so the celebrity may present himself as a new friend because he knows it is a good insurance policy against knocking copy. But never confuse this friendliness for the real thing. You want a story. He or she wants publicity for the product.

It is not only the famous who have something to sell. For years, people talked to the press without pausing to consider that there might be money in what they discussed. Now the most junior witness to a road crash will barely open his mouth without asking what is in it for him.

Papers have only themselves to blame, of course, for the word has got around that they will pay. Some do, some don't. The ones that don't tend to dress up their decision as a matter of morality, but it may well have as much to do with meanness.

Local newspapers tend not to pay, though that doesn't prevent reporters bunging money for drinks at a level they can reclaim on expenses. The so-called quality papers don't like to pay, but that doesn't stop them writing cheques for first-hand exclusive accounts in certain circumstances, and once those accounts are dressed up as a book, they see them entirely differently.

In the popular and middle markets, payments are now routinely made for stories that could give papers a commercial edge. Show-business publicists such as Max Clifford make no secret about bringing together newspapers and their clients who have a story to tell. Indeed, Mr Clifford enjoys the publicity because he knows it will encourage new clients to bring their stories to him. Without this system, the Sunday papers would not be full of 'models' eager to pose on satin sheets and reveal how many times a night they did it with the professional footballers they found in their local nightclub.

You may find that the same lawyers who rail against intrusion into their client's privacy are simultaneously negotiating for their client to talk. At this level, payments are organized through properly drawn up contracts, involving lawyers from both sides. These contracts will stipulate exclusivity, the level of assistance to be given to the paper's reporters, whether there will be pictures and what level of detail will be expected. There will also be clauses that cancel the payments if the accounts cannot be corroborated to the agreed level.

At a more basic level, deals may be more informal. News editors licence senior reporters to agree amounts. A person with a good story to tell may find competing offers – each prepared on paper bearing the newspaper's masthead – dropping through his letterbox. Whether he will get the money he thinks he is getting is another matter.

Fortunately, those who really do have something papers might pay for, often blurt it out before discussing the fee. If they want to become businessmen they must learn how to do business. If they are stupid enough to tell you something, don't think you can't go and write it just because they suddenly believe there is money in what they have witnessed.

Twenty-five years ago, working for the Sheffield *Star*, I remember tracking down the best friend of the prostitute who had been with the mass murderer the Yorkshire Ripper the night he was arrested. The prostitute was to have been the next victim – he had a hammer with him when he was arrested – and the girl I went to see had been soliciting for business on the same street.

She'd talked to her friend and gave a graphic account of what had happened, encouraged by her pimp, sitting alongside her. Late, too late, he suggested the talk must be worth some money. The *Star* doesn't pay for information, I explained, but promised to put him in touch with a man I knew from the *Sun*.

Later I heard that the *Sun* had been round, offered a few hundred pounds for the talk and gone through the whole story. 'Have you got the money, then?' asked the pimp. 'What for?' asked the man from the *Sun*, throwing down a copy of the *Star*. 'There's nothing in this that's not in tonight's paper.'

Who, in a story like that, emerges with his feet on the moral high ground? The reporter from the *Sun* or the man living off the earnings of the prostitute? We are into that territory addressed by Samuel Johnson, when he was asked to judge which of two minor poets was the better. There was no point, he said, in deciding the precedence between a louse and a flea.

So, before we judge journalists too harshly, let us also remember the morality of some of those who deal with them: of the politicians who think they can promote themselves, the businessmen who seek a higher profile, the adulterers who think they can cash in on their sex lives. Heaven knows, there are few enough journalists who are saints. But by no means all of them are sinners.

Dream On I

John Carlin, foreign correspondent, the *Observer*

'Spending a day with George W. Bush, having total access to him from morning till night, he behaving naturally and you allowed to report on everything you see and hear. It would be fascinating, fun and a huge scoop all in one. It would never happen but you did ask for a dream story.'

Charlie Catchpole, television critic, *Daily Express* and *Daily Star*

'Dream story: as a columnist, I don't do real stories any more. But I could retire happily if I got the word from a solid source at the BBC that they were pulling the plug on *EastEnders*.'

Mark Henderson, science correspondent, *The Times* – joined September 1996 as a graduate trainee

'I'm Science Correspondent, so it would have to be the discovery of life on Mars. Anyone who isn't fascinated by the idea that terrestrial life is not alone in the Universe is pretty small-minded. The discovery of life elsewhere in the Solar System would change world views as profoundly as the Copernican revolution, or Columbus's voyage to the New World. It would mean that life, which as far as we know is unique, is actually abundant throughout the Universe. It's not a good-news or bad-news story as such, but one with such philosophical significance that it really puts the day-to-day ephemera of Westminster in perspective.'

11

Who needs paper?

The internet changed the world of information. No other medium can reach so many people, in so many places, in so few seconds. Doesn't that make it the most wonderful opportunity for journalists since the invention of the printing press?

For a while, it looked that way. Newspapers, encouraged by the crazy, South Sea Bubble economics of the late 1990s, suddenly began seriously to believe that their websites were about to be worth many times the value of the papers from which they had sprung. Even on this side of the Atlantic we could sense the shock over at the *New York Times* when reporters were told that the website was now worth billions of dollars, the implication being that an august paper had pretty much had its day. No matter that the paper was a physical thing that people paid money for every day while the internet version was free. Somehow the new economics would take care of all that.

It promised too to set newspaper reporters free. Either that, or remove them from the horror of daily deadlines to the potential greater hell of rolling, instant publishing.

No more would their news coverage be confined to grey words and still pictures supplied to readers twenty-four hours late. Now journalists looked to build a future in which they would be out with video cameras supplying instant news, complete with visual feeds. They would not need the crews and technical equipment of a television station. They could go live to anyone with a computer link.

At the *Daily Telegraph,* the first British paper to create a website, we began discussing which reporters should read the lunchtime bulletin, streamed on broadband.

We all knew radio had failed to kill off papers. And papers had survived television rather marvellously. But this, surely, was the end. Around the turn of the century, I interviewed Steve Ballmer, then the President and later the Chief Executive Officer of Microsoft. Within a few years, he explained, and certainly by the time our children had children, there would be no more paper.

Newspapers had already seen circulation revenue decline as a result of the price wars started by Rupert Murdoch, who appeared to be prepared to sell *The Times* for less than it cost to produce. Now they were making their news available for nothing, on the net. Only the *Wall Street Journal* took the precaution of building a subscription model from the start. Journalists associated with the internet took to swaggering round offices in open-necked shirts – no one connected to the net wore a tie – to the fury of their colleagues. Those involved with the internet were the future and didn't they want the old guys who had stuck with the paper version to know it.

Papers cranked up websites. Independent sites sprang up too, splurging the money they raised from credulous venture capitalists on big salaries for journalists. Universities running journalism degrees introduced courses devoted to the web. This, it was clear, was the future.

In 1999, as the dotcom bubble inflated, I was invited to join a little gang working to import one of the first magazine websites, Slate.com, from the United States. *Slate* was the creation of Microsoft, which was interested in retaining a stake and offering us the chance to run a British franchise, if we could raise several million pounds.

I could not see why a website devoted to current affairs and politics should suddenly be worth multiples of existing paper-and-ink magazines merely by virtue of being on the net. In those days of the emperor's new clothes, it was unhelpful to point such things out. So naturally I kept quiet about these misgivings as we did the round of venture capital houses, many of which were prepared to throw some millions of pounds at the project.

When the *Daily Telegraph* offered me a job, it seemed a better bet to return to old media. It was. The dotcom boom went bust in the following few months. And all those bankers who had talked up internet deals into billions of pounds denied that it had ever been anything to do with them.

That doesn't mean that the internet is no good for journalism. On the contrary. Internet sites reach new audiences and bring a world-wide readership to British papers. They raise a paper's profile and, we are beginning to see, introduce new advertising revenues that suggest sites will soon turn a profit.

And if journalists are unlikely to find the riches from the internet that they first imagined, many will still find good jobs within it. The university courses are still going. Papers are beginning to expand their websites again, confident that good revenues will follow.

The web is a noticeboard to which the entire world has potential access, so that a story posted in Delhi can be read immediately in Lahore or in Moscow; the *Jerusalem Post* can find more online readers in New York City than it has circulation in Israel; a disgruntled spy in Britain can publish his colleagues' names where security agents in China can read them.

Television and radio have a massive audience. *Voice of America* and the BBC World Service achieve near global penetration. The reach of CNN is growing. The satellite empire of Rupert Murdoch expands by the day. All have a broadening reach. But neither radio nor television conveys more than an infinitesimal amount of the information that is available on the Worldwide Web.

Newspapers need printing presses and a means of distribution; radio and television stations require a means of broadcasting. These are expensive. All three media are subject to the close scrutiny and sometimes censorship of the state, whether at point of broadcasting or point of reception.

By contrast, the cost of posting on the internet is tiny and state means of controlling it are few. If you are a frustrated author, publish your work on the net. If newspapers won't take your stories, put them on your own website. Or, if you want to find out what you can't find out from papers for legal reasons, go to the web discussion groups. When several police investigations into allegations of rape by professional footballers began, newspapers were prevented by the libel laws from identifying the suspects. It was the work of minutes to find the names on the internet.

This state of affairs is unlikely to last too long. The net may have started as the kind of anarchic place where anybody could post anything, but the lawyers are catching up fast. They had a problem at first, for there would have been little profit in suing the individuals who leave comments on discussion boards. But there is profit in pursuing the publishers who set up the discussion groups, or the internet service providers who rent them the space or allow access to offending material.

But if the internet is creating new work for lawyers, it is also providing opportunities in news organizations. It may not have been the explosion of jobs that was envisaged in the days of the boom, but things are coming along nicely now. The national papers nearly all have web units, with separate teams of journalists. Nearly all the existing print and broadcast media include the internet in their operations, though they are inconsistent in their reasons for doing so. The BBC's website, for instance, has grown into one of the glories of the world, though commercial publishers argue that it has used too much of the licence payers' money to create it.

Yahoo, one of the top internet search engines, lists more than fifty newspapers in India alone with a web edition, plus eight radio and four television services. Some papers, particularly in the United States, have started publishing editions on the web rather than in print, saving the cost of newsprint and making their profit in advertising revenue.

And if the great dotcom collapse created a greater cynicism about the internet, it did not do it long-term damage. One day, say the serious internet enthusiasts, no one will read papers any more. All information will be read online.

Newspapers will never die, say the traditionalists. Who likes reading on screen? It is fine for quick information, but useless for long pieces. The internet is a gimmick.

Somewhere in between are the publishing pragmatists, who talk about a world in which readers choose the 'platform' on which they receive their news, whether it be paper, digital television, mobile phone or computer screen. This is happening. With improving screen technology I find it no harder to read a 3,000-word feature online than on the page. In the meantime, most publishers see the web as a means of marketing their titles to readers who would not otherwise buy them and achieving advertising revenue for doing so.

In theory, it would appear commercially suicidal to place information on the web for nothing while simultaneously charging for it at the newsstand. I know there are papers I no longer buy because I can read the bits I am interested in on the web. In one of my periodic stints as a freelance writer, early on in the development of the net, I was amazed to find so much free material available in the newspaper archives of the world. Strangely, however, such industry research as is available suggests that papers are not losing buyers by publishing web editions.

Some papers, cautiously, allow only a part of their journalism to appear on the web. Others, bolder, not only publish the lot, but make it available before the paper is even on the streets. In my days as a columnist at the *Daily Telegraph* I became used to receiving emails in the small hours from Americans who had read my work online before the paper was on sale on Britain.

The bold papers are driven, like journalism has to be, by the desire to be first. Once you have set up a website, what is the point in putting old news on it? Newspaper websites find themselves in competition with the radio and television companies, which are used to pumping out live or 'real-time' news. If papers are to compete online, where the audience expects instant news, they have to do the same.

That means that it is no longer enough to publish online their daily edition. They are turning themselves into 24-hour news operations, which means changing traditional work patterns geared to producing a flow of copy aimed at a single edition of the newspaper.

The 2000 Olympics in Sydney, Australia, where time differences meant that newspapers in many parts of the world were printing results and reports hours after readers had heard or seen them became a turning point. Many papers posted reports on the internet before they appeared in the paper. This led to arguments about what material should be held back for paying readers. The typical compromise was that the results went up immediately, but the colour writing by big names was held back for the paper and put on the web only after publication.

Once newspapers start indulging the net, where does it end? It is easy to see how big news stories and sports results must be posted early on the internet, but why not features? And editorials? The challenge of the internet is to rethink the way in which a newspaper and its staff operate. And once you go that far, how long do you persist in the basic rhythm of the newspaper day, which sees stories written at deadlines based on press times?

Such changes are less marked in the world of radio and television, where the media are already used to working around the clock, putting out news as and when it happens. Broadcasters have been quick to put their news on the internet. The BBC has been particularly efficient but has the benefit of being able to draw on its network of staff and special correspondents.

The same is true of news agencies, whose staff are used to filing instant updates, rather than the more considered pieces of newspaper correspondents. Some agencies have toyed with becoming suppliers of news direct to the reader. Most, however, see their future as similar to their past – the supply of news to broadcasters, newspapers and net publishers.

It looks as though the internet will complement rather than destroy printed media, let alone radio and television. But the sheer demand for material – there are no constraints on the amount that can be published – threatens to downgrade what journalism is.

A vulgar word has come into play to describe what is on those sites: 'content'. Where newspaper editors once asked for news stories, or features, or articles for their papers; where broadcasters asked for news bulletins, or programmes, those who run websites demand 'content'.

They have used the term as if it could be bought and sold by the bucketload, or in metre lengths, as if 'content' were merely multiple words and sentences strung together, something to fill all that space. Do you want to be known as a journalist, a reporter, a writer – or a 'content provider'?

But now the older values are reasserting themselves. A new and more sophisticated internet audience is demanding not only all the new technology of the medium but also that there be something of quality to see there. They are looking – as they have always looked in newspapers and magazines – for what is well-written, or new or otherwise interesting or entertaining.

They are also beginning to understand that not everything on the internet is true. I watch my children copying across 'facts' from history sites for school projects and realize how much is wrong. We are used to a culture of newspapers where, while mistakes are made, copy has at least been seen by several pairs of eyes before it appears in black and white. Web production requires no such checks. I can post information on my website that can be picked up by a search engine and passed off as true. You have only to type in a request to a search engine to discover how many different versions of the truth are available on the web, even down to the correct spelling of stars' names. If you are relying on the web for facts, you may be taking a big risk. The natural thing, to be safe, is to go to sites that seem trustworthy – typically, this means to sites run by newspapers or other media that have a good reputation.

The result is that internet journalism is not different from other forms, just because it is possible to publish so much more quickly. The importance of accuracy, relevance and clarity remains. A journalist who can write well for a newspaper, news agency, radio or television station is a journalist who can write well for the net.

That means the main beneficiaries of the web are not new journalists or publications, but existing ones. For the journalist already employed in offline media, there are new rewards. If journalists want more than anything to be read (and watched and listened to), then their copy goes many times further on the internet. For some there may even be the opportunity to negotiate new deals with employers.

If they believe they can be first with the news, then they no longer have to wait for the printing press or the news bulletin. Journalists arrive at their offices these days to find their words dissected on other continents while the paper version is still printing. A correspondent at the scene of a terrorist outrage or natural disaster may file for his or her paper but reach a worldwide audience through the net.

But the internet potentially provides a far greater freedom, in allowing journalists – and anyone else – to publish to the world without the help or hindrance of employer, print works, censor or government. It also creates more job opportunities: if newspapers can publish around the clock, how can they do it without having journalists to work around the clock?

It is easy to publish fast on the internet. Is it too easy? As we discussed in the case of the footballers in Chapter 7, one of the most popular currencies online has been rumour. But putting something in print doesn't make it true. Journalists need to make sure that they apply the checks and balances of their normal work to publishing online.

And just because your words exist only in cyberspace, don't think that the lawyers won't find them there.

12

Reading the readers

The other day I was watching through a two-way mirror as a group of *Daily Telegraph* readers talked about the paper. This is a voyeuristic way to spend an evening, though that is not the only reason I was in two minds about being there. The thing is, most journalists say that any editor who needs a focus group to tell him whether his paper is any good shouldn't be in the business.

It is true that journalists do develop an instinctive feel for the interests of their readership. Paul Dacre of the *Daily Mail* prides himself on it, even though his near-million-pound salary and chauffeur-driven car take him out of the league of most of his readers. But as a child of the North London suburbs, he feels he retains an instant appreciation of the things that make his readers tick.

Sun readers would probably also be surprised to discover how much journalists earn. How do you match up the metropolitan expenses-driven habits of the writers with the very average earnings of the readers? To compensate for this increasing gap, the editor, Rebekah Wade, has taken senior staff to a Butlin's holiday camp so that they can discover how their readers think and live and play. Is that the place to find a representative sample? Ms Wade clearly thinks so.

For newspaper advertising and marketing departments it is vital to get a clear view of the readers, of their age, their social background, their net worth and all those other indicators of use to advertisers. It is also helpful to get an idea of which bits of the paper they like and don't like, because that is information to use as a weapon against journalists who think they know such things instinctively (it would be easy to write a separate chapter on the way in which the advertising departments, the marketing departments and the editorial departments quarrel, each believing the others to be barely competent).

The only external feedback that most journalists get is from friends or relatives, though in my experience you can't even rely on them. Not unless there is some ghastly mistake in the copy, anyway. I have thrilled to the sight of a reader on the Tube turning the page to the very column I have written. Will she notice the picture by-line and look up? No. Invariably, I have subsided as she turns the page without so much as a glance at my work.

The other thing to do is watch readers choosing papers in the newsagent's. Again, the process is usually little comfort. After all the work that goes on each night to create a paper of unique appeal on the news-stand, readers barely seem to waver over the competing front pages before grabbing the one they want, probably the one they came in for.

But their letters are a great source of comfort, even if you can't help noticing how many seem completely to have missed the point you were trying to make. There are certain issues that are guaranteed to set readers off: anything about grammar or clichés or misused words invariably provokes letters giving their own particular pet hates.

But is a big postbag an indication that you have hit on an important issue? Or do some topics merely attract a rather predictable subset of your readership? What about star columnists? Do you need them, on their huge contracts? Instinctively, you think they are a vital part of the mix. Then why is it that when they retire or are sacked or move to another paper, you never get a single letter saying how sorry the reader is that they have gone?

This is always a moment of pure triumph for all those news reporters who believe that they are grossly underpaid compared with the big columnists. 'Has there been a lot of letters about the absence of so and so?' they inquire innocently. 'Not one? Really? Fancy that!'

The subject comes up again when papers debate what single transfer would simultaneously improve their own sale while disrupting that of a rival. When Simon Kelner became editor of the *Independent* his first inclination was to bust his budget by luring A. A. Gill or Jeremy Clarkson from the *Sunday Times*. Then he had a go at getting Boris Johnson from the *Daily Telegraph*. These were figures, according to the buzz, that readers actually recognized.

I think he was right to try, though the relationships these writers had with their papers meant he was almost certainly doomed to fail. Time after time, when asked why they read the *Sunday Times*, people have responded that they like that A. A. Gill, or that you've got to read Clarkson, haven't you? The *Sunday Times* knows this, and looks after them well.

They would be two of the first names on any journalist's list when it comes to that popular pub game, Names That Readers Notice. Most would add Richard Littlejohn from the *Sun*, and perhaps Michael Parkinson at the *Daily Telegraph*. After that they begin to struggle.

Print journalists don't like to admit it, but there is no doubt that a few television appearances greatly enhance a columnist's recognition factor. Having watched focus groups talking about *Telegraph* titles, I am convinced that Anne Robinson, Boris Johnson and Ian Hislop are singled out not just because they are good writers, but also because readers recognize their faces.

Fortunately, there is some justice. Good columnists get noticed if they are also on the telly: poor columnists go unnoticed despite being on television. This heartening information suggests it is not enough just to sign up any dullard who happens to have been on breakfast telly: in order to write a good column, they have to have something to say. The fact that most television people don't becomes clear as soon as they file their first piece.

You can see why it is irresistible to watch readers going through a paper, to hear them say what they do and don't like, even if they do appear to miss half of your favourite pieces. The process also highlights the dangers of being too clever in copy: most readers seem to prefer a statement of the obvious, particularly when it chimes with their own views. You thought you were producing sophisticated articles for an intellectual audience. They thought they were buying a paper that would offer a proper weather map, in colour.

Let me explain the dynamics of the focus group, usually involving half a dozen people at each session, each paid £50 for their time. Depending on the information you are trying to get from them, they will be readers either of your paper or of a rival. Sometimes they have been asked to read specific papers beforehand; sometimes they are given the paper, or dummies of a new look, when they arrive.

They sit around a coffee table with drinks and sandwiches and crisps. A moderator sits with them, guiding the conversations towards the questions he wants answering. Behind the big mirror on the wall is a viewing gallery, in which sit executives from the paper's editorial and marketing departments, picking over a cold buffet and drinking wine. We can hear the focus group. The group can't hear us.

That means we can sigh when they make wholly predictable comments and whoop in triumph when they notice something we hoped they would spot. Pretty quickly we pick out the group members who have least to contribute and most to say. Then we decide on our favourites, the ones who speak most clearly in support of our own notions of what the paper is or should be.

The danger is that such groups only confirm what you already suspect, though that could be because you are properly close to the readers and what they want. The last session I went to was designed to tease out *Daily Telegraph* readers' views of one of the great modern issues of journalism: have papers dumbed down?

Put simply, this is the view that the so-called quality papers no longer write intelligently. They fail to cover serious subjects at a proper length and they write about frothy, superficial, trivial things that should not be in a serious paper.

The decline has occurred too, the argument goes, in the world of magazines. There, titles such as *Marie Claire*, which began with a commitment to serious journalism, have added extra dollops of frivolity, and appeared to reduce the level of painstaking reportage for which it once won rewards. This is a world, remember, where the weekly magazines for men, *Nuts* and *Zoo*, cleaned up by offering their male readers a return to the sex, sport and dirty-joke-obsessed days of their adolescence.

The principal supporters of the dumbing-down thesis are politicians, who argue that papers should cover what Tony Benn, the veteran Labour politician, used to call 'the issues', rather than the personalities. The modern media, they say, avoid discussing important matters in favour of trivializing them through the prism of clashes between different politicians. Papers prefer, for example, to write about the bust-up over a European constitution rather than explain exactly what the terms of that European constitution are.

In the spring of 2004, the journalist Stephen Glover, one of the founders of the *Independent*, announced plans to create a new quality paper in Britain. It would be aimed at the 100,000 readers who had become disenchanted with their own quality titles, because they were now full of show business gossip and television trivia.

The model, he explained, would be intelligent continental papers such as *Le Monde*. Within weeks, as he tried to raise the finance to launch the new paper, he said that more than 100 journalists from the other quality papers had applied to join it. But raising the money proved harder than he imagined.

There is an alternative view to the dumbing-down thesis, which is that papers merely reflect the way that society has changed. Once there were high and low cultures, and the two did not mix. Now people are interested in a much greater range of subjects, some of them entirely trivial, and enjoy reading about them.

This view of the world believes that readers of quality newspapers do want to know if the England football manager is about to break his contract and like to know that a top model has broken off her engagement to a singer.

The alternative view goes on to point out that the educational qualifications of those writing for papers are higher than at any other time – we have discussed elsewhere in this book how bright minds who would once have joined the Civil Service and investment banks now head for journalism – and that the overall standard of writing is higher. There have always been bright leader writers, but now the news reporters have degrees too. Does a degree necessarily mean that you write more intelligently? If only it did.

Leaving that to one side, the counter-argument asserts that politicians who complain do so because they resent anyone writing about their private lives, even though modern politics has encouraged voters to get to know more about the candidates seeking their vote.

In recent years, the battle has intensified over the reporting of two particular television programmes, *I'm a Celebrity, Get Me Out of Here* and *Big Brother*. Both have generated huge audiences, but are they the kind of thing that quality papers should write about?

If you do, you will be accused of dumbing down. If you don't, are you shortchanging your readers, given that half the country becomes obsessed with these shows during the weeks that they run?

In the past the quality papers have just about got away with it by reporting not the shows themselves but the *phenomenon* of the shows. It is a technique that the *Guardian* is particularly good at. It drives the popular papers crazy, because they argue that the *Guardian* is doing no more than they do, but getting away with it by presenting it as a sociological investigation or, when they want to come back to it for a second go, an exercise in irony.

I had begun to believe that the whole of Britain did indeed know about and take some kind of interest in these shows until I happened to attend a dinner at the Tate Gallery one year the night the winner of *I'm a Celebrity* emerged from the jungle. At the end of the dinner our host rose to speak and said he had never heard of the programme in question, but that he had been asked to tell us who had won. About half the guests knew immediately what he was talking about; the other half looked puzzled.

It was easy to see, that night, why many readers of quality papers might be perplexed by news stories referring to popular television programmes they had never watched. Was this what quality papers were for?

The good news from the focus group was that readers did not resent coverage of stories that would once have appeared only in the pops. No, they said, the paper had not dumbed down. It had merely broadened the scope of its reporting. They liked to talk about these shows.

Then what about the puffs, those promotional spaces around the titlepiece on the front of the paper that are used to promote the stories inside? Did these cheapen the appeal of the *Daily Telegraph*? Not at all, it was helpful to get an idea of what was inside. The readers were interested in all kinds of stories, and these puffs encouraged them to read.

The features? The columnists? Didn't they want more news? Far from it. They now expected a daily paper to cover a wide range of stories and to combine revelation, information, humour and entertainment. This was all heartening stuff. If there are readers who believe the quality press has been dumbing down, they weren't in those focus groups that night.

But some things don't change. Did they remember noticing any of the columnists? Had those carefully created picture by-lines made any impression? Not much. There was one they picked out. Annie Robinson. Now, isn't she that woman from the telly?

Dream On II

Paul Rees, editor, *Q* magazine

'On a professional level, the exclusive Eminem interview is currently it. On a personal one a phone call saying, "Of course you can come and spend a week with Bruce Springsteen on his farm" would take the biscuit.'

Jo Elvin, editor, *Glamour* magazine

'As it's hard to be current on a monthly (we work two months ahead of our onsale date), my ideal is wherever possible to have the celebrity story straight from the horse's mouth. This week it would be Victoria Beckham's first interview commenting on David Beckham's alleged infidelities. Next week it will probably be something entirely different! Occasionally we have done that, we had Jennifer Lopez's first interview about Ben Affleck, Britney Spears' first retorts when Fred Durst claimed they'd slept together.'

Ruth Gledhill, religion correspondent, *The Times*

'My dream became a reality when I got the exclusive story on the appointment of the present Archbishop of Canterbury, Dr Rowan Williams. This was down to journalistic hard work, experience and the cultivation of contacts.'

13

Remember this

If you remember nothing else from this book, these three precepts will set you on the right path.

Watch, listen and learn.

A colleague at the *Daily Telegraph* looked wistful when I told him I was writing advice for those looking to make a start in journalism: 'Ah, young talent!' he said. 'What an exciting thing it is to see bright young people making their way up. Every newspaper I have worked on, I have made it my business to discover young talent . . . and ruthlessly snuff it out.'

He was smiling, but he wasn't altogether joking. There are only so many page-one stories to go round and big-name reporters didn't get picture by-lines by giving way to cubs. So don't expect the generation ahead of you to strew rose petals in your path.

On the other hand, most won't actually try to kill you. Journalism is a collaborative process, and as long as you don't arrive looking too pleased with yourself, reporters will welcome you to the team.

Once you are around journalists, pay attention. Become a sponge. You will learn more from watching your colleagues in action than from any course in journalism. Listen to how they deal with people on the phone, watch them on a doorstep, see how they handle an interview. Most of all, read their stories – before and after they are subbed. That way, you learn a lot about what to write and how to write. You also discover that the reputation of some famous reporters owes as much to the sub-editors as to their own ability.

Enjoy any praise that comes your way but concentrate on the criticism. It will do you more good in the long run. The sooner you stop making mistakes, the faster you will move on.

Tune in to the office buzz. Learn what is going on. Watch the ones on their way up and work out how they are getting on – and why others are not. Why do some reporters' stories never stand up to close scrutiny? Who cuts corners and makes free with facts? Why does she always scream down the phone? How does he find addresses so quickly?

Absorb it all, from the best shorthand pencil to buy, to the quickest way to ask a grieving mother to give up a picture of her dead son. The lessons are all around you, every day. There's no quicker way to learn. And remember: just because a reporter is more experienced than you, it doesn't mean he or she is necessarily right. Watch it all – and remember the techniques that work.

GIVE ME ENERGY AND ENTHUSIASM

I don't want to play the grumpy old man, but when did young people around a newspaper office decide that mundane tasks were beneath them? The first day I walked into a national newspaper office, I expected to be sent out for the teas: now we get work-experience sixth-formers at the *Daily Telegraph* who think they will be writing the splash by 4 o'clock.

The other day a trainee objected when he was asked to transcribe a tape of an interview conducted by one of the paper's most senior journalists. 'This isn't the kind of work I came here to do,' he said. By the time the editor had finished with him, the abject apology he was told to write to the senior journalist was splashed with tears.

So show that you want to work. Reporters who make light of small jobs find themselves taking on bigger jobs. The mundane research you are doing for the investigative reporter today could be a working partnership tomorrow. And worry about the hours you are working when you are older. For now, make yourself available for everything.

Everyone prefers to work with colleagues who can think of a way to make a story work rather than three reasons why it won't. Somebody is going to crack that story. Start off with the philosophy that it is going to be you.

Sure, the bounce may wear off in time. You'll have bad days when it is hard to come back for more. But it is the journalists who show drive who move up quickest. I can think of some senior colleagues who bring the enthusiasm of a wet flannel to every piece they write, but they have to have double the talent to get away with it.

There are enough sub-editors to make bad writers better. But if we don't have journalists with the passion to dig up stories, we haven't got a newspaper business.

WRITE IN PLAIN ENGLISH

Why make it harder for yourself and the reader? Remember that you are writing for people who do not have your close knowledge of a subject. Build your stories in a logical way and in an English that all can understand.

Sub-editors can save you from disaster, but the more clearly you write, the more likely that your story will impress those first, crucial newspaper executives who read it. Otherwise, busy news editors may decide that the piece you have filed is just too much trouble to unscramble. If you can't be bothered to write clearly, why should anyone be bothered to read what you have written?

DO UNTO OTHERS . . .

You should not need the law and the Press Complaints Commission to remind you of your responsibilities. Do not use the competitive world of newspapers as an excuse for lying and cheating, for treating the population at large as cannon fodder for stories, for destroying lives that need never have come to public attention. Newspapers haven't got a reputation for irresponsibility by chance, but because journalists have chosen to act in a particular way.

That doesn't mean you should not be rude, ill-tempered, bad-mannered, challenging, cynical, patronizing, aggressive, hectoring, abusive, bullying or any other adjective you fancy. It does mean you should choose the people or the subjects that deserve those treatments.

If you are going to make journalism your life, then make it a life you can be proud of. Take all the froth and fun that you want. But remember that you follow in a tradition of press freedom that is still denied in many countries around the world. You may not choose to see the serious side, but are signing on as a watchdog of our democratic freedoms.

PART 3

THE CONTACTS

National Newspapers

Daily Express
Ludgate House, 245 Blackfriars Road, London SE1 9UX
☎ 020 7928 8000   Fax 020 7620 1654
Website www.express.co.uk

Owner *Northern & Shell Media/Richard Desmond*
Editor *Peter Hill*

Circulation 942,171

Daily Mail
Northcliffe House, 2 Derry Street, London W8 5TT
☎ 020 7938 6000
Website www.dailymail.co.uk

Owner *Associated Newspapers/Lord Rothermere*
Editor *Paul Dacre*

Circulation 2.4 million

Daily Mirror
1 Canada Square, Canary Wharf, London E14 5AP
☎ 020 7293 3000   Fax 020 7293 3409
Website www.mirror.co.uk

Owner *Trinity Mirror plc*
Editor *Richard Wallace*

Circulation 1.91 million

Daily Record
One Central Quay, Glasgow G3 8DA
☎ 0141 309 3000   Fax 0141 309 3340
Website www.record-mail.co.uk

Owner *Trinity Mirror plc*
Editor *Bruce Waddell*

Circulation 503,077

Daily Sport
19 Great Ancoats Street, Manchester M60 4BT
☎ 0161 236 4466   Fax 0161 236 4535
Website www.dailysport.co.uk

Owner *Sport Newspapers Ltd*
Editor *David Beevers*

Circulation 200,000

Daily Star
Ludgate House, 245 Blackfriars Road, London SE1 9UX
☎ 020 7928 8000   Fax 020 7922 7960
Email dailystarnewsdesk@dailystar.co.uk
Website www.mediauk.com

Owner *Northern & Shell Media/ Richard Desmond*
Editor *Dawn Neesom*

Circulation 903,702

Daily Star Sunday

Ludgate House, 245 Blackfriars Road, London SE1 9UX

☎ 020 7928 8000   Fax 202 7922 7960

Owner *Northern & Shell Media/ Richard Desmond*
Editor *Gareth Morgan*

Circulation 551,000

Daily Telegraph

1 Canada Square, Canary Wharf, London E14 5DT

☎ 020 7538 5000   Fax 020 7513 2506

Website www.telegraph.co.uk

Owner *Telegraph Ltd/ Barclay Brothers*
Editor *Martin Newland*

Circulation 923,042

Financial Times

1 Southwark Bridge, London SE1 9HL

☎ 020 7873 3000   Fax 202 7873 3076

Email feedback@customercare.ftdirect.com
Website www.ft.com

Owner *Pearson*
Editor *Andrew Gowers*

Circulation 401,000

Guardian

119 Farringdon Road, London EC1R 3ER

☎ 020 7278 2332   Fax 202 7837 2114

Website www.guardian.co.uk

Owner *The Scott Trust*
Editor *Alan Rusbridger*

Circulation 376,287

Herald (Glasgow)
200 Renfield Street, Glasgow G2 3PR
☎0141 302 7000   Fax 0141 302 7070
Website www.theherald.co.uk

Owner *Gannett UK Ltd*
Editor *Mark Douglas-Home*

Circulation 83,083

Independent
Independent House, 191 Marsh Wall, London E14 9RS
☎020 7005 2000   Fax 020 7005 2999
Website www.independent.co.uk

Owner *Independent Newspapers*
Editor *Simon Kelner*

Circulation 258,012

Independent on Sunday
Independent House, 191 Marsh Wall, London E14 9RS
☎020 7005 2000   Fax 020 7005 2999

Owner *Independent Newspapers*
Editor *Tristan Davies*

Circulation 209,236

International Herald Tribune
6 bis, rue des Graviers, 92521 Neuilly, Paris
☎0033 1 4143 9300   Fax 0033 1 4143 9338 (editorial)
Email iht@iht.com
Website www.iht.com

Circulation 245,223

Mail on Sunday

Northcliffe House, 2 Derry Street, London w8 5TS

☎ 020 7938 6000   Fax 020 7937 3829

Owner *Associated Newspapers/Lord Rothermere*
Editor *Peter Wright*

Circulation 2.38 million

Morning Star

William Rust House, 52 Beachy Road, London E3 2NS

☎ 020 8510 0815   Fax 020 8986 5694

Email morsta@geo2.poptel.org.uk

Website www.morningstar.com

Owner *Peoples Press Printing Society*
Editor *John Haylett*

Circulation 9,000

News of the World

1 Virginia Street, London E98 1NW

☎ 020 7782 1000   Fax 020 7583 9504

Website www.newsoftheworld.co.uk

Owner *News International plc/Rupert Murdoch*
Editor *Andy Coulson*

Circulation 3.95 million

Observer

119 Farringdon Road, London EC1R 3ER

☎ 020 7278 2332   Fax 020 7713 4250

Email editor@observer.co.uk

Website www.observer.co.uk

Owner *Guardian Newspapers Ltd*
Editor *Roger Alton*

Circulation 452,257

The People

1 Canada Square, Canary Wharf, London E14 5DT

☎ 020 7293 3614   Fax 020 7293 3887

Email feedback@mirror.co.uk

Website www.people.co.uk

Owner *Trinity Mirror plc*
Editor *Mark Thomas*

Circulation 1.02 million

Scotland on Sunday

Barclay House, 108 Holyrood Road, Edinburgh EH8 8AS

☎ 0131 620 8620   Fax 0131 620 8491

Website www.scotlandonsunday.com

Owner *Scotsman Publications Ltd*
Editor *John McLellan*

Circulation 83,952

Scotsman

Barclay House, 108 Holyrood Road, Edinburgh EH8 8AS

☎ 0131 620 8620   Fax 0131 620 8616 (editorial)

Website www.scotsman.com

Owner *Scotsman Publications Ltd*
Editor *Iain Martin*

Circulation 70,656

The Sun

1 Virginia Street, London E98 1SN

☎ 020 7782 4100   Fax 020 7782 4108

Email firstname.lastname@the-sun.co.uk

Website www.the-sun.co.uk

Owner *News International plc/Rupert Murdoch*
Editor *Rebekah Wade*

Circulation 3.3 million

Sunday Express

Ludgate House, 245 Blackfriars Road, London SE1 9UX

☎ 020 7928 8000   Fax 020 7620 1654

Website www.express.co.uk

Owner *Northern & Shell Media/ Richard Desmond*
Editor *Martin Townsend*

Circulation 952,171

Sunday Herald

200 Renfield Street, Glasgow G2 3QB

☎ 0141 302 7800   Fax 0141 302 7815

Email editor@sundayherald.com

Website www.sundayherald.com

Owner *Newsquest*
Editor *Andrew Jaspan*

Circulation 58,303

Sunday Mail

One Central Quay, Glasgow G3 8DA

☎ 0141 309 3000   Fax 0141 309 3587

Website www.sundaymail.co.uk

Owner *Trinity Mirror plc*
Editor *Allan Rennie*

Circulation 605,743

Sunday Mirror
1 Canada Square, Canary Wharf, London E14 5AP
☎ 020 7293 3000   Fax 020 7293 3939 (news desk)
Website www.sundaymirror.co.uk
Owner *Trinity Mirror*
Editor *Tina Weaver*

Circulation 1.58 million

Sunday Post
2 Albert Square, Dundee DD1 9QJ
☎ 01382 223131   Fax 01382 201064
Email mail@sundaypost.com
Website www.sundaypost.com
Owner *D.C Thomson & Co. Ltd*
Editorial *David Pollington*

Circulation 530,168

Sunday Sport
19 Great Ancoats Street, Manchester M60 4BT
☎ 0161 236 4466   Fax 0161 236 4535
Website www.sundaysport.com
Owner *David Sullivan*
Editor *Paul Carter*

Circulation 178,740

Sunday Telegraph

1 Canada Square, Canary Wharf, London E14 5DT

☎ 020 7538 5000   Fax 020 7538 6242

Website www.telegraph.co.uk

Owner *Telegraph Ltd/ Barclay Brothers*
Editor *Dominic Lawson*

Circulation 697,771

Sunday Times

1 Pennington Street, London E98 1XY

☎ 020 7782 5000   Fax 020 7782 5658

Website www.sunday-times.co.uk

Owner *News International plc/Rupert Murdoch*
Editor *John Witherow*

Circulation 1.4 million

The Times

1 Pennington Street, London E98 1TT

☎ 020 7782 5000   Fax 020 7488 3242

Website www.thetimes.co.uk

Owner *News International plc/Rupert Murdoch*
Editor *Robert Thomson*

Circulation 658,637

Regional Newspapers

Cambridgeshire
Cambridge Evening News
Winship Road, Milton, Cambridge CB4 6PP
☎ 01223 434434   Fax 01223 434415
Owner *Cambridge Newspaper Ltd*
Editor *Colin Grant*

Circulation 34,619

Co. Durham
Northern Echo
Priestgate, Darlington DL1 1NF
☎ 01325 381313   Fax 01325 380539
Email echo@nne.co.uk
Website www.thisisthenortheast.co.uk
Owner *Newsquest (North East) Ltd (a Gannett company)*
Editor *Peter Barron*

Circulation 56,447

Greater London
Evening Standard

Northcliffe House, 2 Derry Street, London w8 5EE

☎ 020 7938 6000   Fax 020 7937 2648

Website www.standard.co.uk/e-editions

Owner *Associated Newspapers/Lord Rothermere*
Editor *Veronica Wadley*

Circulation 393,887

Lancashire
Lancashire Evening Post

Olivers Place, Eastway, Fulwood, Preston PR2 9ZA

☎ 01772 254841   Fax 01772 880173

Website www.prestontoday.net

Owner *Johnston Press plc*
Editor *Simon Reynolds*

Circulation 44,876

Merseyside
Liverpool Echo

PO Box 48, Old Hall Street, Liverpool L69 3EB

☎ 0151 227 2000   Fax 0151 236 4682

Email letters@liverpoolecho.co.uk

Website www.icliverpool.icnetwork.co.uk

Owner *Trinity Mirror Merseyside*
Editor *Mark Dickinson*

Circulation 135,845

Norfolk
Eastern Daily Press
Prospect House, Rouen Road, Norwich NR1 1RE
☎ 01603 628311   Fax 01603 623872
Website www.EDP24.co.uk

Owner *Archant Regional*
Editor *Peter Franzen*

Circulation 72,323

Somerset
Evening Post
Temple Way, Bristol BS99 7HD
☎ 0117 934 3000   Fax 0117 934 3575
Email mail@epost.co.uk
Website www.epost.co.uk

Owner *Bristol United Press plc*
Editor *Mike Lowe*

Circulation 59,000

Sussex
The Argus
Argus House, Crowhurst Road, Hollingbury, Brighton BN1 8AR
☎ 01273 544544   Fax 01273 505703
Email simonb@atheargus.co.uk
Website www.thisisbrightonandhove.co.uk

Owner *Newsquest (Sussex) Ltd*
Editor *Simon Bradshaw*

Circulation 42,464

West Midlands
Birmingham Evening Mail

PO Box 78, Weaman Street, Birmingham B4 6AT

☎ 0121 236 3366

Email eveningmail@mrn.co.uk

Owner *Trinity Mirror Plc*
Editor *Roger Borrell*

Circulation 107,410

Express & Star

Queen Street, Wolverhampton WV1 1ES

☎ 01902 313131   Fax 01902 319721

Owner *Midlands News Association*
Editor *Adrian Faber*

Circulation 163,543

Yorkshire
Hull Daily Mail

Blundell's Corner, Beverly Road, Hull HU3 1XS

☎ 01482 327111

Email news@hulldailymail.co.uk

Website www.thisishull.co.uk

Owner *Northcliffe Newspapers Group Ltd*
Editor *John Meehan*

Circulation 71,337

The Star

York Street, Sheffield S1 1PU

☎ 0114 276 7676   Fax 0114 272 5978

Owner *Sheffield Newspapers Ltd*
Editor *Peter Charlton*

Circulation 75,881

Yorkshire Evening Post
Wellington Street, Leeds LS1 1RF
☎ 0113 243 2701   Fax 0113 238 8536
Email eped@ypn.co.uk
Owner *Johnson Press*
Editor *Neil Hodgkinson*

Circulation 81,116

NORTHERN IRELAND

Belfast Telegraph
Royal Avenue, Belfast BT1 1EB
☎ 028 9026 4000   Fax 028 9055 4506/4540
Owner *Independent News & Media (UK)*
Editor *Edmund Curran*

Circulation 108,651

SCOTLAND

The Press and Journal
PO Box 43, Lang Stracht, Mastrick, Aberdeen AB15 6DF
☎ 01224 690222   Fax 01224 663575
Owner *Northcliffe Newspapers Group Ltd*
Editor *Derek Tucker*

Circulation 90,379

WALES

Daily Post

PO Box 202, Vale Road, Llandudno Junction, Conwy LL31 9ZD
☎ 01492 574455   Fax 01492 574433
Email welshnews@dailypost.co.uk

Owner *Trinity Mirror Plc*
Editor *in Chief Alastair Machray*

Circulation 47,000

South Wales Argus

Cardiff Road, Maesglas, Newport NP20 3QN
☎ 01633 810000   Fax 01633 777202
Website www.thisisgwent.co.uk

Owner *Newsquest*
Editor *Gerry Keighley*

Circulation 30,700

The Western Mail

Thomson House, Havelock Street, Cardiff CF10 1XR
☎ 029 2058 3583   Fax 029 208 3652
Website www.icwales.com

Owner *Trinity Mirror Plc*
Editor *Alan Edmunds*

Circulation 44,559

CHANNEL ISLANDS

Guernsey Press & Star

Braye Road, Vale, Guernsey GY1 3BW
☎ 01481 240240   Fax 01481 240235
Email newsroom@guernsey-press.com
Website www.guernsey-press.com

Owner *Guiton Group*
Editor *Richard Digard*

Circulation 16,411

Jersey Evening Post

PO Box 582, Jersey JE4 8XQ
☎ 01534 611611   Fax 01534 611622
Email editorial@jerseyeveningpost.com
Website www.thisisjersey.com

Owner *Jersey Evening Post Ltd*
Editor *Chris Bright*

Circulation 22,492

Magazines

Architects' Journal
151 Rosebery Avenue, London EC1R 4GB
☎ 020 7505 6700   Fax 020 7505 6701
Website www.ajplus.co.uk

Owner *Emap Construct*
Editor *Isabel Allen*

Circulation 16,441

Arena
Endeavour House, 189 Shaftesbury Avenue, London WC2H 8JG
☎ 020 7437 9011

Owner *Emap East*
Editor *Anthony Noguera*

Circulation 40,617

Attitude
Northern & Shell Tower, City Harbour, 4 Selsdon Way,
London E14 9GL
☎ 020 7308 5261   Fax 020 7308 5384
Email attitude@attitudemag.co.uk

Owner *Remnant Media*
Editor *Adam Mattera*

Circulation 60,000

BBC Gardeners' World Magazine

Woodlands, 80 Wood Lane, London w12 0TT
☎ 020 8433 3959   Fax 020 8433 3986
Email adam.pasco@bbc.co.uk

Owner *BBC Worldwide Publishing Ltd*
Editor *Adam Pasco*

Circulation 285,772

BBC Good Food

Woodlands, 80 Wood Lane, London w12 0TT
☎ 020 8433 2000   Fax 020 8433 3931
Email goodfood.magazine@bbc.co.uk

Owner *BBC Worldwide Publishing Ltd*
Editorial *Director Gillian Carter*

Circulation 325,000

BBC Top Gear Magazine

Top Gear, Room 4356, BBC White City, 201 Wood Lane,
London w12 7TS
☎ 020 8433 3716   Fax 020 8433 3754
Website www.topgear.com

Owner *BBC Worldwide Ltd*
Editor *Michael Harvey*

Circulation 136,216

Best

72 Broadwick Street, London W1F 9EP
☎ 020 7439 5000   Fax 020 7312 4175
Email best@natmags.co.uk

Owner *National Magazine Company*
Editor *Louise Court*

Circulation 420,437

Big Issue

1–5 Wandsworth Road, London SW8 2LN
☎ 020 7526 3200   Fax 020 7526 3201
Email editorial@bigissue.com
Website www.bigissue.com

Editorial-in-Chief *A. John Bird*
Editor *Matt Ford*

Circulation 122,679

Birds

RSPB, The Lodge, Sandy SG19 2DL
☎ 01767 680551   Fax 01767 683262
Email rob.hume@rspb.org.uk
Website www.rspb.org.uk

Owner *Royal Society for the Protection of Birds*
Editor *R.A. Hume*

Circulation 618,174

Black Beauty & Hair

2nd Floor, Culvert House, Culvert Road, Battersea,
London SW11 5HD
☎ 020 7720 2108   Fax 020 7498 3023

Email info@blackbeautyandhair.com
Website www.blackbeautyandhair.com

Owner *Hawker Consumer Publications Ltd*
Editor *Irene Shelly*

Circulation 21,500

Bliss Magazine

Endeavour House, 189 Shaftesbury Avenue, London WC2H 8JG
☎ 020 7208 3478   Fax 020 7208 3591
Email alex.thwaites@emap.com

Owner *Emap élan*
Editor *Helen Johnston*

Circulation 241,664

Boyz

2nd Floor, Medius House, 63–69 New Oxford Street,
London WC1A 1DG
☎ 020 7845 4300   Fax 020 7845 4309
Email hudson@boyz.co.uk

Editor *David Hudson*

Circulation 55,000

Brides

Vogue House, Hanover Square, London W1S 1JU
☎ 020 7499 9080   Fax 020 7152 3369

Owner *Condé Nast Publications Ltd*
Editor *Liz Savage*

Circulation 66,000

Chat

IPC Media Ltd., King's Reach Tower, Stamford Street, London SE1 9LS

☎ 020 7261 6565   Fax 020 7261 6534

Website www.ipcmedia.com/magazines/chat

Owner *IPC Connect*
Editor *June Smith-Sheppard*

Circulation 604,582

Company

National Magazine House, 72 Broadwick Street, London W1F 9EP

☎ 020 7439 5000   Fax 020 7312 3797

Email company.mail@natmags.co.uk

Website www.company.co.uk

Owner *National Magazine Co. Ltd*
Editor *Victoria White*

Circulation 331,000

Computer Weekly

Quadrant House, The Quadrant, Sutton SM2 5AS

☎ 020 8652 3122   Fax 020 8652 8979

Email computer.weekly@rbi.co.uk

Website www.computerweekly.com

Owner *Reed Business Information*
Editor *Hooman Bassirian*

Circulation 143,000

Condé Nast Traveller

Vogue House, Hanover Square, London W1S 1JU

☎ 020 7499 9080   Fax 020 7493 3758

Email editorcntraveller@condenast.co.uk
Website www.cntraveller.co.uk

Owner *Condé Nast Publications*
Editor *Sarah Miller*

Circulation 83,000

CosmoGIRL!
National Magazine House, 72 Broadwick Street, London W1F 9EP
☎ 020 7439 5000   Fax 020 7439 5400
Email cosmogirl.mail@natmags.co.uk
Website www.cosmogirl.co.uk

Owner *National Magazine Co Ltd*
Editor *Celia Duncan*

Circulation 198,324

Cosmopolitan
National Magazine House, 72 Broadwick Street, London W1F 9EP
☎ 020 7439 5000   Fax 020 7439 5016
Email cosmo.mail@natmags.co.uk
Website www.cosmopolitan.co.uk

Owner *National Magazine Co. Ltd*
Editor *Sam Baker*

Circulation 460,665

Country Life
IPC Media Ltd., King's Reach Tower, Stamford Street,
London SE1 9LS
☎ 020 7261 7058   Fax 020 7261 5139
Website www.countrylife.co.uk

Owner *IPC Media*
Editor *Clive Aslet*

Circulation 42,649

Country Living

National Magazine House, 72 Broadwick Street, London W1F 9EP
☎ 020 7439 5000   Fax 020 7439 5093
Website www.countryliving.co.uk

Owner *National Magazine Co. Ltd*
Editor *Susy Smith*

Circulation 175,000

Dazed & Confused

112 Old Street, London EC1V 1BD
☎ 020 7336 0766   Fax 020 7336 0966
Email dazed@confused.co.uk
Website www.confused.co.uk

Owner *Waddell Ltd*
Editor *Callum McGeoch*

Circulation 80,000

Disability Now

6 Market Road, London N7 9PW
☎ 020 7619 7323   Fax 020 7619 7331
Email editor@disabilitynow.org.uk
Website www.disabilitynow.org.uk

Owner *SCOPE*
Editor *Mary Wilkinson*

Circulation 20,000

Diva, lesbian life and style

Spectrum House, 32–34 Gordon House Road, London NW5 1LP

☎ 020 7424 7400   Fax 020 7424 7401

Email edit@divamag.co.uk

Website www.divamag.co.uk

Owner *Millivers-Prowler Ltd*

Editor *Jane Czyzselska*

Eastern Eye

Unit 2, 65 Whitechapel Road, London E1 1DU

☎ 020 7650 2000   Fax 020 7650 2001

Website www.ethnicmedia.co.uk

Website www.easterneyeuk.co.uk

Owner *Ethnic Media Group*

Editor *Amar Singh*

Circulation 40,000

The Economist

25 St James's Street, London SW1A 1HG

☎ 020 7830 7000   Fax 020 7839 2968

Website www.economist.com

Owner *Pearson/individual shareholders*

Editor *Bill Emmott*

Circulation 146,401 (UK)

The Edge

65 Guinness Buildings, Hammersmith, London W6 8BD

☎ 020 8563 1310

Email davec@theedge.abelgratis.co.uk

Website www.theedge.abelgratis.co.uk

Editor *Dave Clark*

Elle

64 North Row, London W1K 7LL

☎ 020 7150 7000   Fax 020 7150 7670

Owner *Hachette Filipacchi*
Editor *Lorraine Candy*

Circulation 201,309

Empire

4th Floor, Mappin House, 4 Winsley Street, London W1W 8HF

☎ 020 7436 1515   Fax 020 7343 8703

Email empire@emap.com

Website www.empireonline.co.uk

Owner *Emap East*
Editor *Colin Kennedy*

Circulation 190,659

Esquire

National Magazine House, 72 Broadwick Street, London W1F 9EP

☎ 020 7439 5000   Fax 020 7439 5675

Owner *National Magazine Co. Ltd*
Editor *Simon Tiffin*

Circulation 70,164

Essentials

IPC Media Ltd., King's Reach Tower, Stamford Street, London SE1 9LS

☎ 020 7261 6970   Fax 0207 261 5262

Owner *IPC Media*
Editor *Karen Livenmore*

Circulation 150,402

FHM
Mappin House, 4 Winsley Street, London W1W 8HF
☎ 020 7436 1515   Fax 020 7343 3000
Email general@fhm.com
Website www.fhm.com

Owner *Emap Plc*
Editor *David Davies*

Circulation 601,166

The Garden, Journal of the Royal Horticultural Society
RHS Publications, 4th Floor, Churchgate New Road,
Peterborough PE1 1TT
Email thegarden@rhs.org.uk
Website www.rhs.org.uk

Owner *The Royal Horticultural Society*
Editor *Ian Hodgson*

Circulation 306,000

Gay Times
Unit M, Spectrum House, 32–34 Gordon House Road,
London NW5 1LP
☎ 020 7424 7400   Fax 020 7424 7401
Website www.gaytimes.co.uk

Owner *Millivers-Prowler Group*
Editor *Vicky Powell*

Circulation 65,000

Girl About Town
Independent House, 191 Marsh Wall, London E14 9RS
☎ 020 7005 5550   Fax 020 7005 5777

Email gat@indmags.co.uk
Website www.londoncareers.net

Owner *Independent Magazines*
Editor-in-Chief *Bill Williamson*

Circulation 85,000

Glamour
6–8 Old Bond Street, London w1s 4ph
☎ 020 7499 9089   Fax 020 7491 2551
Website www.glamourmagazine.co.uk
Website www.condenast.co.uk

Owner *Conde Nast*
Editor *Jo Elvin*

Circulation 582,690

Golf Monthly
IPC Media Ltd., King's Reach Tower, Stamford Street,
London se1 9ls
☎ 020 7261 7237   Fax 020 7261 7240
Email golfmonthly@ipcmedia.com
Website www.golf-monthly.co.uk

Owner *IPC media*
Editor *Jane Carter*

Circulation 75,000

Good Housekeeping
National Magazine House, 72 Broadwick Street, London w1f 9ep
☎ 020 7439 5000   Fax 020 7439 5616
Email firstname.lastname@natmags.co.uk
Website www.natmags.co.uk

Owner *National Magazine Co. Ltd*
Editor-in-Chief *Lindsay Nicholson*

Circulation 415,730

Hair

IPC Media Ltd., Kings Reach Tower, Stamford Street,
London SE1 9LS
☎ 020 7261 6974   Fax 020 7261 7382
Website www.ipcmedia.com/magazines/hair

Owner *IPC Media*
Editor *Zoe Richards*

Circulation 157,499

Harpers & Queen

National Magazine House, 72 Broadwick Street, London W1F 9EP
☎ 020 7439 5000   Fax 020 7439 5506
Website www.harpersandqueen.co.uk

Owner *National Magazine Co. Ltd*
Editor *Lucy Yeomans*

Circulation 90,227

Heat

Endeavour House, 189 Shaftesbury Avenue, WC2H 8JG
☎ 020 7437 9011   Fax 020 7859 8670
Email heat@emap.com

Owner *Emap Entertainment*
Editor *Mark Frith*

Circulation 567,000

Hello!

Wellington House, 69–71 Upper Ground, London SE1 9PQ
☎020 7667 8700   Fax 020 7667 8716
Website www.hellomagazine.com

Owner *Hola! (Spain)*
Editor *Ronnie Whelan*
Commissioning Editor *Linda Newman*

Circulation 350,374

Homes & Gardens

IPC Media Ltd., King's Reach Tower, Stamford Street,
London SE1 9LS
☎020 7261 5000   Fax 020 7261 6247
Website www.homesandgardens.com

Owner *IPC media*
Editor *Deborah Barker*

Circulation 162,817

Horse and Hound

IPC Media Ltd., King's Reach Tower, Stamford Street,
London SE1 9LS
☎020 7261 6315   Fax 020 7261 5429
Email jenny_sims@ipcmedia.com

Owner *IPC media*
Editor *Lucy Higginson*

Circulation 68,320

House & Garden

Vogue House, Hanover Square, London W1S 1JU
☎020 7499 9080   Fax 020 7629 2907

Website www.condenast.co.uk
Website www.houseandgarden.co.uk

Owner *Conde Nast Publications Ltd*
Editor *Susan Crewe*

Circulation 148,716

House Beautiful
National Magazine House, 72 Broadwick Street, London W1F 9EP
☎ 020 7439 5000   Fax 020 7439 5141

Owner *National Magazine Co. Ltd*
Editor *Kerryn Harper*

Circulation 182,025

i-D Magazine
124 Tabernacle Street, London EC2A 4SA
☎ 020 7490 9710 F020 7251 2225
Email editor@i-dmagazine.co.uk
Website www.i-dmagazine.com

Owner *Levelprint*
Editor *Avril Mair*

Circulation 66,000

Ideal Home
IPC Media Ltd., King's Reach Tower, Stamford Street,
London SE1 9LS
☎ 020 7261 6505   Fax 020 7261 6697
Email firstname_surname@ipcmedia.com

Owner *IPC Media*
Editor *Susan Rose*

Circulation 274,488

It's Hot! Magazine

Rm A1136, BBC Worldwide, Woodlands, 180 Wood Lane, London W12 0TT

☎ 020 8433 2447   Fax 020 8433 2763

Email itshot@bbc.co.uk

Owner *BBC Worldwide*
Editor *Peter Hart*

Circulation 116,515

Jewish Chronicle

25 Furnival Street, London EC4A 1JT

☎ 020 7415 1500   Fax 020 7405 9040

Email editorial@thejc.com

Website www.thejc.com

Owner *Kessler Foundation*
Editor *Edward J. Temko*

Circulation 50,000

Kerrang!

Mappin House, 4 Winsley Street, London W1N 7AR

☎ 020 7436 1515   Fax 020 7182 8910

Website www.kerrang.com

Owner *Emap Performance*
Editor *Ashley Bird*

Circulation 69,261

Literary Review

44 Lexington Street, London W1F 0LW

☎ 020 7437 9392 f 020 7734 1844

Email litrev@dircon.co.uk

Editor *Nancy Sladek*

Circulation 15,000

Loaded

IPC Media Ltd., King's Reach Tower, Stamford Street,
London SE1 9LS
☎ 020 7261 5562   Fax 020 7261 5557
Email andrew_woods@ipcmedia.com
Website www.loaded.co.uk

Owner *IPC media*
Editor *Martin Daubney*
Features Editor *Andrew Woods*

Circulation 263,108

Management Today

174 Hammersmith Road, London W6 7JP
☎ 020 8267 5000
Website www.clickmt.com
Email management.today@haynet.com

Owner *Haymarket Business Publications Ltd*
Editor *Matthew Gwyther*

Circulation 102,000

marie claire

13th Floor, King's Reach Tower, Stamford Street, London SE1 9LS
☎ 020 7261 5240   Fax 020 7261 5277
Email marieclaire@ipcmedia.com
Website www.ipcmedia.com

Owner *European Magazines Ltd*
Editor *Marie O'Riordan*

Circulation 360,789

Maxim

30 Cleveland Street, London W1T 4JD
☎ 020 7907 6410   Fax 020 7907 6439
Email editorial@maxim-magazine.co.uk
Website www.maxim-magazine.co.uk

Owner *Dennis Publishing*
Editor *Greg Gutfield*

Circulation 243,341

Men's Health

7–10 Chandos Street, London W1G 9AD
☎ 020 7291 6000   Fax 020 7291 6053
Website www.menshealth.co.uk

Owner *Rodale Publishing*
Editor *Morgan Rees*

Circulation 220,446

Mojo

Mappin House, 4 Winsley Street, London W1W 8HF
☎ 020 7436 1515   Fax 020 7312 8296
Email mojo@emap.com
Website www.mojo4music.com

Owner *Emap-Metro*
Editor-in Chief *Phil Alexander*

Circulation 104,437

Moneywise

RD Publications Ltd, 11 Westferry Circus, Canary Wharf,
London E14 4HE
☎ 020 7715 8465   Fax 020 7715 8733
Website www.moneywise.co.uk

Owner *Reader's Digest Association*
Editor *Ben Livesy*

Circulation 105,000

More!

Endeavour House, 189 Shaftesbury Avenue, WC2H 8JG
☎ 020 7208 3165   Fax 020 7208 3595
Email abby.woolf@emap.com
Website www.moremagazine.co.uk

Owner *Emap élan Publications*
Editor *Alison Hall*

Circulation 260,000

Motor Cycle News

Media House, Lynchwood, Peterborough Business Park,
Peterborough PE2 6EA
☎ 01733 468000   Fax 01733 468028
Email MCN@emap.com
Website www.motorcylenews.com

Owner *Emap plc*
Editor *Marc Potter*

Circulation 141,914

National Trust Magazine

36 Queen Anne's Gate, London SW1H 9AS
☎ 020 7222 9251   Fax 020 7222 5097
Email enquiries@thenationaltrust.org.uk

Owner *The National Trust*
Editor *Gaynor Aaltonen*

Circulation 1.47 million

New Internationalist
55 Rectory Road, Oxford OX4 1BW
☎ 01865 728181   Fax 01865 793152
Email ni@newint.org
Website www.newint.org

Owner *New Internationalist Trust*
Co-Editors *Vanessa Baird, David Ransom, Katharine Ainger, Adam Ma'anit*

Circulation 80,000

New Nation
Unit 2, 65 Whitechapel Road, London E1 1DU
☎ 020 7650 2000   Fax 020 7650 2001
Website www.ethnicmedia.co.uk

Owner *Ethnic Media Group*
Editor *Michael Eboda*

Circulation 30,000

New Scientist
1st Floor, 151 Wardour Street, London W1F 8WE
☎ 020 8652 3500   Fax 020 7331 2772 (News)
Website www.newscientist.com

Owner *Reed Business Information Ltd*
Editor-in-Chief *Dr Alun Anderson*
Editor *Jeremy Webb*

Circulation 143,902

New Statesman
New Statesman, 3rd Floor, 52 Grosvenor Gardens,
London SW1W 0AU
☎ 020 7730 3444   Fax 020 7259 0181
Website www.newstatesman.com

Publisher *Spencer Neal*
Editor *Peter Wilby*

Circulation 25,000

New Woman

Endeavour House, 189 Shaftesbury Avenue, WC2H 8JG
☎ 020 7437 9011 Fax 020 7208 3585
Email kate.turner@emap.com
Website www.newwoman.co.uk

Owner *Emap élan Ltd*
Editor *Sara Cremer*

Circulation 291,000

OK! Magazine

Ludgate House, 245 Blackfriars Road, London SE1 9UX
☎ 020 7928 8000 Fax 020 7579 4607
Email firstname.lastname@express.co.uk

Owner *Northern & Shell Media/Richard Desmond*
Editor *Lisa Palta*

Circulation 571,000

Press Gazette

Quantum House, 19 Scarbrook Road, Croydon CR9 1LX
☎ 020 8565 4473 Fax 020 8565 4395
Email pged@pressgazette.co.uk
Website www.pressgazette.co.uk

Owner *Quantum*
Editor *Ian Reeves*
Deputy Editor *Jon Slattery*

Circulation 9,500

Pride

Hamilton House, 55 Battersea Bridge Road, London SW11 3AX

☎ 020 7228 3110   Fax 020 7228 3129

Email info@pride.com

Owner *Carl Cushnie Junior*
Editor *Amina Taylor*

Circulation 40,000

Prima

National Magazine House, 72 Broadwick Street, London W1F 9EP

☎ 020 7439 5000

Email prima@natmags.co.uk

Website www.natmags.co.uk

Owner *National Magazine Company*
Editor *Maire Fahey*

Circulation 330,000

Private Eye

6 Carlisle Street, London W1D 3BN

☎ 020 7437 4017   Fax 020 7437 0705

Email strobes@private-eye.co.uk

Website www.private-eye.co.uk

Owner *Pressdram*
Editor *Ian Hislop*

Circulation 205,250

Prospect
2 Bloomsbury Square, London WC1A 2QA
☎ 020 7255 1344 (editorial)/1281 (publishing)   Fax 020 7255 1279
Email editorial@prospect-magazine.co.uk or publishing@prospect-magazine.co.uk
Website www.prospect-magazine.co.uk

Owner *Prospect Publishing Limited*
Editor *David Goodhart*

Circulation 24,400

Q-News, The Muslim Magazine
55 Bryanston Street, London W1H 7AJ
☎ 020 7859 8217   Fax 020 7868 8600
Email info@qnews.com

Owner *Faud Namdi*
Editor *Shagufta Yaqub*

Circulation 15,000

Racing Post (incorporating The Sporting Life)
1 Canada Square, Canary Wharf, London E14 5AP
☎ 020 7293 3000   Fax 020 7293 3758
Email editor@racingpost.co.uk
Website www.racingpost.co.uk

Owner *Trinity Mirror plc*
Editor *Chris Smith*

Radio Times
80 Wood Lane, London W12 0TT
☎ 0870 608 4455   Fax 020 8433 3160
Email radio.times@bbc.co.uk
Website www.radiotimes.com

Owner *BBC Worldwide Limited*
Editor *Gill Hudson*

Circulation 1.16 million

Reader's Digest
11 Westferry Circus, Canary Wharf, London E14 4HE
☎ 020 7715 8000   Fax 020 7715 8716
Website www.readersdigest.co.uk

Owner *Reader's Digest Association Ltd*
Editor-in-Chief *Katherine Walker*

Circulation 860,000

Runner's World
Natmag-Rodale Limited, 33 Broadwick St, London W1F 0DQ
Email editor@runnersworld.co.uk
Website www.runnersworld.co.uk

Owner *Rodale Press*
Editor *Steven Seaton*

Circulation 70,206

Safeway: The Magazine
Redwood, 7 Saint Martin's Place, London WC2N 4HA
☎ 020 7747 0788   Fax 020 7747 0799

Editor *Jennifer Newton*

Circulation 1.8 million

Saga Magazine
Saga Publishing Ltd, The Saga Building, Enbrook Park,
Folkstone CT20 3SE
☎ 01303 771526   Fax 01303 776699
Website www.saga.co.uk

Owner *Saga Publishing Ltd*
Editor *Emma Soames*

Circulation 1.19 million

Sainsbury's Magazine
20 Upper Ground, London SE1 9PD
Email edit@newcrane.co.uk

Owner *New Crane Publishing*
Editor *Sue Robinson*
Consultant Food Editor *Delia Smith*

Circulation 278,043

Shooting and Conversation
BASC, Marford Mill, Rossett, Wrexham LL12 0HL
☎ 01244 573000   Fax 01244 573001
Website www.basc.org.uk

Owner *The British Association for Shooting and Conservation (BASC)*
Editor *Jeffery Olstead*

Circulation 120,000

Smash Hits
Mappin House, 4 Winsley Street, London W1W 8HF
☎ 020 7436 1515   Fax 020 7636 5792
Email letters@smashhits.net
Website www.smashhits.net

Owner *Emap Performance*
Editor *Lisa Smosarski*

Circulation 114,383

The Spectator
56 Doughty Street, London WC1N 2LL
☎ 020 7405 1706   Fax 020 7242 0603
Email editor@spectator.co.uk
Website www.spectator.co.uk

Owner *The Spectator (1828) Ltd*
Editor *Boris Johnson*

Circulation 63,223

The Stage (incorporating Television Today)
Stage House, 47 Bermondsey Street, London SE1 3XT
☎ 020 7403 1818   Fax 020 7357 9287
Email editor@thestage.co.uk
Website www.thestage.co.uk

Owner *The Stage Newspaper Ltd*
Editor *Brian Attwood*

Circulation 41,500

Sugar Magazine
64 North Row, London W1K 7LL
☎ 020 7150 7050   Fax 020 7150 7678
Website www.sugarmagazine.co.uk

Owner *Hachette Filipacchi (UK)*
Editor *Nick Chalmers*
Editorial *Director Lysanne Currie*

Circulation 291,794

Take a Break
Academic House, 24–28 Oval Road, London NW1 7DT
☎ 020 7241 8000
Email tab.features@bauer.co.uk

Owner *H. Bauer Publishing Ltd*
Editor *John Dale*

Circulation 1.25 million

Tatler

Vogue House, Hanover Square, London w1s 1ju
☎ 020 7499 9080   Fax 020 7409 0451
Website www.tatler.co.uk

Owner *Condé Nast Publications Ltd*
Editor *Geordie Greig*

Circulation 84,330

Time

Brettenham House, Lancaster Place, London wc2e 7tl
☎ 020 7499 4080
Email edit-office@timemagazine.com
Website www.timeeurope.com

Owner *Time Warner*
Editor *(Europe, Middle East, Africa) Eric Pooley*

Circulation 597,038 (Europe)

Time Out

Universal House, 251 Totterham Court Road, London w1t 7ab
☎ 020 7813 3000   Fax 020 7813 6001
Website www.timeout.com

Publisher *Lesley Gill*
Editor *Laura Lee Davies*

Circulation 86,000

Times Educational Supplement

Admiral House, 66–68 East Smithfield, London E1W 1BX

☎ 020 7782 3000   Fax 020 7782 3200

Email newsdesk@tes.co.ukor editor@tes.co.uk

Website www.tes.co.uk

Owner *News International*
Editor *Bob Doe*

Circulation 118,000

Times Higher Education Supplement

Admiral House, 66–68 East Smithfield, London E1W 1BX

☎ 020 7782 3000   Fax 020 7782 3300

Email editor@thes.co.uk

Website www.thes.co.uk

Owner *News International*
Editor *John O'Leary*

Circulation 26,000

Total Film

99 Baker Street, London W1U 6FP

☎ 020 7317 2600   Fax 020 7317 0275

Email totalfilm@futurenet.co.uk

Owner *Future Publishing*
Editor *Matt Mueller*

Circulation 90,580

Traveller

45–49 Brompton Road, London SW3 1DE

☎ 020 7589 0500   Fax 020 7581 1357

Website www.traveller.org.uk

Owner *Wexas International*
Editor *Jonathan Lorie*
Deputy Editor *Amy Sohanpaul*

Circulation 37,000

TVTimes

IPC Media Ltd., King's Reach Tower, Stamford Street,
London SE1 9LS
☎ 020 7261 7000   Fax 020 7261 7888

Owner *IPC media*
Editor *Mike Hollingsworth*

Circulation 524,131

Vogue

Vogue House, Hanover Square, London W1S 1JU
☎ 020 7499 9080   Fax 020 7408 0559
Website www.vogue.co.uk

Owner *Conde Nast Publications Ltd*
Editor *Alexandra Shulman*

Circulation 202,259

The Voice Newspaper

Blue Star House, 234–244 Stockwell Road, London SW9 9UG
☎ 020 7737 7377   Fax 020 7274 8994
Email newsdesk@the-voice.co.uk
Website www.voice-online.co.uk

Managing Director *Linda McCalla*
Group Editor *Deidre Forbes*

Circulation 40,000

Wasafiri

Dept of English & Drama, Queen Mary College, University of
London, Mile End Road, London E1 4NS
☎ 020 7882 3120   Fax 020 7882 3120
Email wasafiri@qmul.ac.uk
Website www.wasafiri.org

Editor *Susheila Nasta*
Managing Editor *Richard Dyer*
Reviews Editor *Mark Stein*

What Car?

60 Waldegrave Road, Teddington TW11 8LG
☎ 020 8267 5683   Fax 020 8267 5750
Email whatcar@haynet.com
Website www.whatcar.com

Owner *Haymarket Motoring Publications Ltd*
Editor *Rob Aheme*

Circulation 137,411

What Hi-Fi? Sound & Vision

38–42 Hampton Road, Teddington TW11 0JE
☎ 020 8943 5000   Fax 020 8267 5019
Website www.whathifi.com

Owner *Haymarket Magazines Ltd*
Managing Director *Kevin Costello*
Editor *Clare Newsome*

Circulation 76,000

Woman's Own
IPC Media Ltd., King's Reach Tower, Stamford Street,
London SE1 9LS
☎ 020 7261 5500   Fax 020 7261 5346

Owner *IPC Media*
Editor *Elsa McAlonan*
Features Editor *Jackie Hatton*

Circulation 478,687

Young Voices
Voice Group Limited, Blue Star House, 234–244 Stockwell Road,
London SW9 9UG
☎ 020 7737 7377   Fax 020 7274 8994
Website www.young-voices.co.uk

Managing Director *Linda McCalla*
Group Editor *Deidre Forbes*
Editor *Emelia Kenlock*

Zembla Magazine
61a Ledbury Road, London W11 2AL
☎ 020 7221 8878
Email mail@zemblamagazine.com
Website www.zemblamagazine.com

Owners *Simon Finch, Dan Crowe*
Editor *Dan Crowe*

Circulation 30,000

Zest
National Magazine House, 72 Broadwick Street, London W1F 9EP
☎ 020 7439 5000   Fax 020 7312 3750

Email zest.mail@natmags.co.uk
Website www.zest.co.uk

Owner *National Magazine Company*
Editor *Alison Pylkkanen*
Deputy Editor *Rebecca Frank*

Circulation 105,000

News Agencies

Associated Press Limited

12 Norwich Street, London EC4A 1BP

☎ 020 7353 1515   Fax 020 7353 8118 (Newsdesk)

Material is either generated in-house or by regulars. Hires the occasional stringer. No unsolicited mss.

Dow Jones Newswires

10 Fleet Place, London EC4M 7QN

☎ 020 7842 9900   Fax 020 7842 9361

A real-time financial and business newswire operated by Dow Jones & Co., publishers of The Wall Street Journal. No unsolicited material.

Hayters Teamwork Sports Agency

Image House, Station Road, London N17 9LR

☎ 020 8808 3300   Fax 020 8808 1122

Email sport@haytersteamwork.com

Contact *Nick Johnson*

Provides written/broadcast coverage of sport in the South Yorkshire area.

National News Press and Photo Agency

4–5 Academy Buildings, Fanshaw Street, London N1 5LQ
☎ 020 7684 3000   Fax 020 7684 3030
Email news@nationalnews.co.uk

All press releases are welcome. Most work is ordered or commissioned. Coverage includes courts, tribunals, conferences, general news, etc as well as PR.

Press Association Ltd

292 Vauxhall Bridge Road, London SW1V 1AE
☎ 020 7963 7000/7830 (Newsdesk)   Fax 020 7963 7192 (Newsdesk)
Email copy@pa.press.net
Website www.pa.press.net

No unsolicited material. Most items are produced in-house though occasional outsiders may be used. A phone call to discuss specific material may lead somewhere 'but this is rare'.

Reuters

85 Fleet Street, London EC4P 4AJ
☎ 020 7250 1122

No unsolicited materials.

Solo Syndication Ltd

17–18 Hayward's Place, London EC1R 0EQ
☎ 020 7566 0360   Fax 020 7566 0388
Email tyork@atlanticsyndicaton.com

Founded 1978. Specialises in worldwide newspaper syndication of photos, features and cartoons. Professional contributors only.

Space Press News and Pictures
Bridge House, Blackburn Lane, Goostrey CW4 8PZ
☎01477 533403   Fax 01477 535756
Email Scoop2001@aol.com

Editor *John Williams*
Pictures *Emma Williams*

Founded 1972. Press and picture agency covering the North West and North Midlands, serving national, regional and local press, TV, radio, and digital picture transmission. Copy and pictures produced for in-house publications and PR. Property, countryside and travel writing.

Press Cutting Agencies

Durrants

Discovery House, 28–42 Banner Street, London EC1Y 8QE

☎ 020 7674 0200   Fax 020 7674 0222

Email contact@durrants.co.uk

Website www.durrants.co.uk

Wide coverage of all print media sectors plus Internet, newswire and broadcast monitoring; foreign press in association with agencies abroad.

International Press Cutting Bureau

224–236 Walworth Road, London SE17 1JE

☎ 020 7708 2113   Fax 020 7701 4489

Email ipcb2000@aol.com

Contact *Robert Podro*

Covers national, provincial, trade, technical and magazine press.

Romeike Media Intelligence

Romeike House, 290–296 Green Lanes, London N13 5TP

☎ 0800 289 543   Fax 020 8882 6716

Email info@romeike.com

Website www.romeike.com

Contact *Alistair Hails*

Monitors national and international dailies and Sundays, provincial paper, consumer magazines, trade and technical journals, teletext services as well as national radio and TV networks, Back research, advertising checking and Internet monitoring.

Xtreme Information

891–2 Worship Street, London EC2A 2BF

☎ 020 7377 1742   Fax 020 7377 6103

Email info@news.xtremeinfomation.com

Website www.news.xremeinformation.com

National and European press monitoring agency.

Bursaries, Fellowships and Grants

The Economist/Richard Casement Internship

The Economist, 25 St James's Street, London sw1a 1hg

☎ 020 7830 7000

Website www.economist.com

Contact *Science Editor*

For an aspiring journalist under 25 to spend three months in the summer writing for The Economist about science and technology. Applicants should write a letter of introduction along with an article of approximately 600 words suitable for inclusion in the Science and Technology section. Competition details normally announced in the magazine late January or early February and 4–5 weeks allowed for application.

Fulbright Awards

The Fulbright Commission, Fulbright House, 62 Doughty Street, London wc1n 2jz

☎ 020 7404 6880   Fax 020 7404 6834

Website www.fulbright.co.uk

Contact *British Programme Manager*

The Fulbright Commission has a number of scholarships given at postgraduate level and above, open to any field (science and the arts) for study/research to be undertaken in the USA. Length of award is typically an academic year. Application deadline for postgraduate awards is usually late October/early November of preceding year of study; and mid-March/ early April for distinguished scholar awards. Further details and application forms are available on the Commission's website. Alternatively, send A4 envelope with sufficient postage for 100g with a covering letter explaining which level of award is of interest.

Guardian Research Fellowship

Nuffield College, Oxford OX1 1NF

☎ 01865 288540   Fax 01865 278676

Contact *The Administrative Officer*

One year fellowship endowed by the Scott Trust, owner of the *Guardian*, to give someone working in the media the chance to put their experience into a new perspective, publish the outcome and give a *Guardian* lecture. Applications welcomed from journalists and management members, in newspapers, periodicals or broadcasting. Research or study proposals should be directly related to experience of working in the media. Accommodation and meals in college will be provided and a stipend. Advertised biennially in November.

Newspaper Press Fund

Dickens House, 35 Wathen Road, Dorking RH4 1JY

☎ 01306 887511   Fax 01306 888212

Email enquiries@preefund.org.uk

Director/Secretary *David Ilott*

Aims to relieve distress among journalists and their dependants. Continuous and/or occasional financial grants; also retirement homes for eligible beneficiaries. Further information and subscription details available from the Director.

Laurence Stern Fellowship

Department of Journalism, City University, Northampton Square, London EC1V OHB

☎020 7040 8224   Fax 020 7040 8594

Website www.city.ac.uk/journalism

Contact *Bob Jones*

FOUNDED 1980. Awarded to a young journalist experienced enough to work on national stories, giving them the chance to work on the national desk of the *Washington Post*. Benjamin Bradlee, the *Post*'s Vice-President-at-Large, selects from a shortlist drawn up in March/April. Full details available on the website.

Useful Websites

British Association of Picture Libraries and Agencies (BAPLA)
Website www.bapla.org.uk

Free telephone referrals available from the BAPLA database through this website.

British Council
Website www.britishcouncil.org

Information on the Council's English Language services, education programmes, science and health links, and information exchange.

British Library
Website www.bl.uk

Reader service enquiries access to main catalogues, information on collections, links to the various Reading Rooms and exhibitions.

Daily Mirror
Website www.mirror.co.uk

The *Daily Mirror* newspaper online.

Electronic Telegraph

Website www.telegraph.co.uk

The *Daily Telegraph* online.

Encyclopaedia Britannica

Website www.eb.com

Subscription access to the entire Encyclopaedia Britannica database as well as Merriam Webster's Collegiate Dictionary and the Britannica Book of the year. EB online also gives links to more than 130,000 sites selected, rated and reviewed by Britannica editors.

Financial Times

Website www.ft.com

The *Financial Times* online.

Frankfurt Book Fair

Website www.frankfurt-book-fair.com/en/portal.thtml

Provides latest news and market analysis of the book business plus information on the Book Fair.

Guardian

Website www.guardian.co.uk

The *Guardian* and the *Observer* newspapers online.

Hansard

Website www.parliament.uk/hansard/hansard.cfm

The official record of debates and written answers in the House of Commons. The transcript of each day's business appears at noon on the following weekday.

Independent

Website www.independent.co.uk

The *Independent* newspaper online.

Journalism UK

Website www.journalismuk.co.uk

A website for UK-based journalists who write for text-based publications. Includes links to newspapers, magazines, e-zines, news sources plus information on jobs, training and organisations.

Society for Freelance Editors and Proofreaders (SFEP)

Website www.sfep.org.uk

The Sun

Website www.thesun.co.uk

The *Sun* newspaper online.

The Times

Website www.thetimes.co.uk

The Times newspaper online.

Webster Dictionary/Thesaurus

Website www.m-w.com

Merriam-Webster Online. Includes a search facility for words in the Webster Dictionary or Webster Thesaurus; word games, 'Word of the Day' and Language Information Zone.

Professional Associations

Association of British Science Writers
Wellcome Wolfson Building, 165 Queen's Gate, London sw7 5HE
☎ 0870 770 3361
Email absw@absw.org.uk
Website www.absw.org.uk

Chairman *Pallab Ghosh*
Administrator *Barbara Drillsma*

Membership £40 (Full) p.a.; £36 (Associate); £5 (Student)

Association of Freelance Journalists
2 Glen Cottage, Brick Hill Lane, Ketley, Telford TF2 6SB
Email afj_info@yahoo.com
Website www.afj.home-page.org

Official Patron *Dr Carl Chinn, PhD, MBE*
Founding President *Martin Scholes*

Subscription £30 p.a.

British Association of Journalists
89 Fleet Street, London EC4Y 1DH
☎ 020 7353 3003   Fax 020 7353 2310

General Secretary *Steve Turner*

Subscription: National newspaper staff, national broadcasting staff, national news agency staff £17.50 a month. Other seniors, including magazine journalists, PRs and freelances: £10 a month. Journalists under 24: £7.50 a month.

British Guild of Travel Writers
12 Askew Crescent, London w12 9DW
☎ 020 8749 1128   Fax 020 8749 1128
Email charlotte.c@virualnecessities.com
Website www.bgtw.org
Chairman *Melissa Shales*
Secretariat *Charlotte Copeman*
Subscription: £100 p.a.

Chartered Institute of Journalists
2 Dock Offices, Surrey Quays Road, London se16 2xu
☎ 020 7252 1187   Fax 020 7323 2302
Email memberservices@ioj.co.uk
Website www.ioj.co.uk
General Secretary *Dominic Cooper*
Subscription £190 p.a.; £16 (monthly)

Foreign Press Association in London
11 Carlton House Terrace, London sw1y 5AJ
☎ 020 7930 0445   Fax 020 7925 0469
Email secretariat@foreign-press.org.uk
Website www.foreign-press.org.uk
General Manager *Bob Jenner*
Membership: £153 p.a. (Full); £142 (Associate Journalists); £215 (Associate Non-Journalists)

Guild of Agricultural Journalists

Isfield Cottage, Church Road, Crowborough TN6 1BN
☎ 01892 611618   Fax 01892 613394
Email don.gomery@farmingline.com
Website www.gaj.org.uk

Honorary General Secretary *Don Gomery*

Subscription £40 p.a.

The Guild of Food Writers

48 Crabtree Lane, London sw6 6LW
☎ 020 7610 1180   Fax 020 7610 0299
Email gfw@gfw.co.uk
Website www.gfw.co.uk

Administrator *Christina Thomas*

Subscription £70

Medical Journalists' Association

Fairfield, Cross in Hand, Heathfield TN21 0SH
☎ 01435 868786   Fax 01435 865714
Email pigache@globalnet.co.uk
Website www.mja-uk.org

Subscription: £30 p.a.

National Union of Journalists

Headland House, 308 Gary's Inn Road, London WC1X 8PD
☎ 020 7278 7916   Fax 020 7837 8143
Email acorn.house@nuj.org.uk
Website www.nuj.org.uk

General Secretary *Jeremy Dear*

Subscription: £177 p.a. (freelance) or 1% of annual income if lower; or 0.5% if income is less than £13,600 p.a.

The Newspaper Society

Bloomsbury House, 74–77 Great Russell Street, London WC1B 3DA

☎ 020 7636 7014   Fax 020 7631 5119

Email ns@newspapersoc.org.uk

Website www.newspapersoc.org.uk

Director *David Newell*

Society for Editors and Proofreaders (SfEP)

1 Riverbank House, 1 Putney Bridge Approach, London SW6 3JD

☎ 020 7736 3318/7736 0901 (Training Dept)   Fax 020 7736 3318

Email administration@sfep.org.uk

Website www.sfep.org.uk

Chair *Naomi Laredo*
Vice-Chair *Penny Williams*

Subscription: £67.50 p.a. (individuals) plus £25 joining fee; corporate membership available.

Society of Editors

University Centre, Granta Place, Mill Lane, Cambridge CB2 1RU

☎ 01223 304080   Fax 01233 304090

Email info@societyofeditors.org

Website www.societyofeditors.org

Executive Director *Bob Satchwell*

Society of Women Writers & Journalists

Calvers Farm, Thelverton, Diss IP21 4NG

☎ 01379 740550   Fax 01379 741716

Email zoe@zoeking.com

Website www.swwj.co.uk

Honorary Secretary *Zoe King*

Subscription: £35 (Town); £30 (Country); £25 (Overseas); £15 joining fee.

Sports Journalists' Association of Great Britain
c/o Sport England Events, 3rd Floor, Victoria House, Bloomsbury
Square, London WC1B 4SE
☎ 020 7273 1789   Fax 020 7383 0273
Email trevjanbond1@aol.com
Website www.sportsjournalists.org.uk

Secretary *Trevor Bond* (244 Perry Street, Billericay CM12 0QP
☎ 01277 651708)

Subscription: £23.50 p.a. (London); £11.75 (Regional).

Prizes

British Press Awards
Press Gazette, Quantum House, 19 Scarbrook Road, Croydon
CR9 1LX
☎020 8565 3056   Fax 020 8565 4395
Email andreah@quantumbusinessmedia.com
Website www.britishpressawards.com

'The Oscars of British journalism.' Open to all British morning and Sunday newspapers sold nationally and to news agencies. March event. Run by Press Gazette.

British Sports Journalism Awards
See **Sports Journalists' Association of Great Britain** *under* **Professional Associations.**

Promoted jointly with Sport England, alongside the British Sports Personalities of the Year Awards, and the Sports Photographer of the Year.

James Cameron Award
City University, Department of Journalism, Northampton Square, London EC1V 0HB
☎020 7040 8221   Fax 020 7040 8594

Contact *The Administrator*

Annual award made to a reporter working for the British media, whose work is judged to have contributed most during the year to the continuance of the City University Department of Journalism.

Martha Gellhorn Trust Prize

Rutherfords, Herbert Road, Salcombe, Devon TQ8 8HN

Annual prize for journalism in honour of one of the twentieth century's greatest reporters. Open to journalism published in English, giving 'the view from the ground – a human story that penetrates the established version of events and illuminates an urgent issue buried by prevailing fashions of what makes news'. Six copies of each entry should be sent to the above address by early March. Prize: £5,000.

Glenfiddich Food & Drink Awards

C/o Wild Card PR, Kenilworth House, 79–80 Margaret Street, London W1W 8TA

Website www.glenfiddich.com/foodanddrink

Known as the 'Cooker Bookers', these awards aim to recognise excellence in writing, publishing and broadcasting on the subjects of food and drink. There are twelve categories for work published or broadcast in the UK and Ireland.

Sir William Lyons Award

The Guild of Motoring Writers, 39 Beswick Avenue, Ensbury Park, Bournemouth BH10 4EY

☎ 01202 518808   Fax 01202 518808

Email gensec@gomw.co.uk

Website www.guildofmotoringwriters.co.uk

Contact *Patricia Lodge*

An annual competitive award aimed at encouraging young people in automotive journalism and at fostering interests in motoring and the motor industry. Entry is by two essays and an interview with Awards Committee. Applicants must be British, aged 17–23 and resident in UK. Final entry date: 30 September.

The Orwell Prize

Alive Events, Fulton House, Fulton Road, Wembley Park HA9 OTF
☎ 020 8584 0444   Fax 020 8584 0443
Email orwell@aliveevents.co.uk
Website www.aliveevents.co.uk

Contact *Sue Dowsett*

Jointly established in 1993 by the George Orwell Memorial Fund and the Political Quarterly to encourage and reward writing in the spirit of Orwell's 'What I have most wanted to do . . . is to make political writing into an art'. Two categories: book or pamphlet; newspaper and/or articles, features, columns, or sustained reportage on a theme in non-fiction or fiction. Submissions by editors, publishers or authors. Prizes: £1,000 for each category.

OWG Awards for Excellence

Outdoor Writers' Guild, PO Box 118, Twickenham TW1 2XB
☎ 020 8538 9468   Fax 020 8538 9468
Website www.owg.org.uk

Contact *Hazelle Jackson*

Established 1980. Annual awards by the Outdoor Writers' Guild to raise the standard of outdoor writing, journalism, broadcasting and photography. Winning categories include guidebook, outdoor book, feature (one-off), feature (regular), photography. Open to OWG members only. Final entries: May.

Pulitzer Prizes

The Pulitzer Prize Board, 709 Journalism Building, Columbia University, 2950 Broadway, New York, NY 10027, USA
☎ 001 212 854 3841   Fax 001 212 854 3342
Email Pulitzer@www.pulitzer.org
Website www.pulitzer.org

Awards for journalism in US newspapers, and for published literature, drama and music by American nationals.

Regional Press Awards

Press Gazzette, Quantum House, 19 Scarbrook Road, Croydon CR9 1LX
☎ 020 8565 3056   Fax 020 8565 4462
Email andreah@quantumbusinessmedia.com

Comprehensive range of journalist and newspaper awards for the regional press. Five newspapers of the year, by circulation and frequency, and a full list of journalism categories. Open to all regional journalists, whether freelance or staff. July event. Run by the Press Gazzette.

Renault UK Journalist of the Year Award

Guild of Monitoring Writers, 39 Beswick Avenue, Ensbury Park, Bournemouth BH10 4EY
☎ 01202 518808   Fax 01202 518808
Email gensec@gomw.co.uk
Website www.guildofmotoringwriters.co.uk

Contact *Patricia Lodge*

Originally the Pierre Dreyfus Award and established 1977. Awarded annually by Renault UK Ltd in honour of Pierre Dreyfus, president director general of Renault 1955–75, to the member of the Guild of Monitoring Writers who is judged to have made the most outstanding journalistic effort in any medium during the year. Particular emphasis placed on initiative and endeavour.

Science Writer Awards

The *Daily Telegraph*, 1 Canada Square, Canary Wharf,
London E14 5AP
☎ 020 7538 6257   Fax 020 7513 2512
Email enquiries@science-writer.co.uk
Website www.science-writer.co.uk

Contact *Emma Gilbert-Harris*

ESTABLISHED 1987, this award is designed to bridge the gap between
science and writing, challenging the writer to come up with a piece of no
more than 700 words that is friendly, informative and, above all, under-
standable. Sponsored by BASF, the award is open to two age groups: 16–19
and 20–28.

Award winners and runners-up receive cash prizes and have the opportunity to have their pieces published on the science pages of the *Daily
Telegraph*. The winner in each category also gets an all expenses paid trip
to the USA for the meeting of the American Association for the Advance-
ment of Science and an invitation to meet Britain's most distinguished
scientists at the British Association's Festival of Science.

Vogue Talent Contest

Vogue, Vogue House, Hanover Square, London W1S 1JU
☎ 020 7152 3003   Fax 020 7408 0559

Contact *Frances Bentley*

Established 1951. Annual award for young writers and journalists (under
25 on 1 January in the year of the contest). Final entry date is in April.
Entrants must write three pieces of journalism on given subjects.

Prizes: £1,000 plus a month's paid work experience with *Vogue*; £500 (2nd).

Index

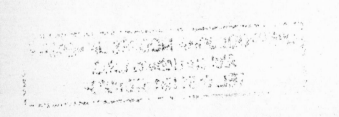